STRAIGHTFORWARD HISTORY

WORLD WAR II

THE DEADLIEST CONFLICT IN HUMAN HISTORY

R.M. CHESTER

WW2: THE DEADLIEST CONFLICT IN HUMAN HISTORY

© Copyright 2023 by R.M. CHESTER — All rights reserved.

This document is geared towards providing exact and reliable information in regards to the topic and issue covered. The publication is sold with the idea that the publisher is not required to render accounting, officially permitted, or otherwise, qualified services. If advice is necessary, legal or professional, a practised individual in the profession should be ordered.

- From a Declaration of Principles which was accepted and approved equally by a Committee of the American Bar Association and a Committee of Publishers and Associations.

In no way is it legal to reproduce, duplicate, or transmit any part of this document in either electronic means or in printed format. Recording of this publication is strictly prohibited and any storage of this document is not allowed unless with written permission from the publisher. All rights reserved.

The information provided herein is stated to be truthful and consistent, in that any liability, in terms of inattention or otherwise, by any usage or abuse of any policies, processes, or directions contained within is the solitary and utter responsibility of the recipient reader. Under no circumstances will any legal responsibility or blame be held against the publisher for any reparation, damages, or monetary loss due to the information herein, either directly or indirectly.

Respective authors own all copyrights not held by the publisher.

The information herein is offered for informational purposes solely, and is universal as so. The presentation of the information is without contract or any type of guarantee assurance.

The trademarks that are used are without any consent, and the publication of the trademark is without permission or backing by the trademark owner. All trademarks and brands within this book are for clarifying purposes only and are the owned by the owners themselves, not affiliated with this document.

WW2: THE DEADLIEST CONFLICT IN HUMAN HISTORY

CONTENTS

INTRODUCTION..9

ROOTS OF THE WAR..11

    CHAPTER I: THE AFTERMATH OF WWI IN EUROPE.........................12
    CHAPTER II: THE RISE OF TOTALITARIANISM................................24
    CHAPTER III: THE APPEASEMENT POLICY AND THE OUTBREAK OF WAR..31
    CHAPTER IV: TROUBLE IN THE EAST...42

THE WAR IN EUROPE..52

    CHAPTER V: THE PHONEY WAR..53
    CHAPTER VI: THE FIRST MAJOR GERMAN OFFENSIVES..............56
    CHAPTER VII: THE BATTLE OF BRITAIN..65
    CHAPTER VIII: OPERATION BARBAROSSA..73
    CHAPTER IX: THE GREEK OFFENSIVE...95
    CHAPTER X: THE NORTH AFRICAN CAMPAIGN.............................110
    CHAPTER XI: THE STATE OF EUROPE 1943......................................122
    CHAPTER XII: THE ALLIES STRIKE BACK..138
    CHAPTER XIII: THE ITALIAN FALLOUT...162
    CHAPTER XIV: THE END OF WAR IN EUROPE..................................175

THE WAR IN THE PACIFIC...181

    CHAPTER XV: THE ROAD TO WAR..182
    CHAPTER XVI: SIX MONTHS TO WIN...193
    CHAPTER XVII: TURNING OF THE TIDES...208
    CHAPTER XVIII: THE MANHATTAN PROJECT.................................228

THE IMPACTS OF WAR..245

    CHAPTER XIX: THE HOLOCAUST..247

- CHAPTER XX: THE REFUGEE CRISIS 277
- CHAPTER XXI: ROLE OF WOMEN 291

THE AFTERMATH OF WAR 305

- CHAPTER XXII: THE UNITED NATIONS 307
- CHAPTER XXIII: POST WAR GERMANY 318
- CHAPTER XXIV: POST WAR JAPAN 338
- CHAPTER XXV: POST WAR ITALY 355
- CHAPTER XXVI: THE POST WAR ALLIES 369
- CHAPTER XXVII: REMEMBERING THE WAR THAT CHANGED THE WORLD 388

AUTHOR'S NOTES 392

STRAIGHTFORWARD HISTORY

INTRODUCTION

Welcome and thank you for purchasing this book "WWII: TRIUMPHS, TRAGEDIES AND THE ENDURING LEGACY OF THE DEADLIEST CONFLICT IN HUMAN HISTORY". This is the first book in the STRAIGHTFORWARD HISTORY series that simplifies the most pivotal moments in human history.

My book on World War II is the perfect choice for anyone looking to gain a deeper understanding of this crucial period. With its detailed exploration of the political, social, and military factors that led to the war, this book provides a comprehensive overview of the key events, battles, and people involved.

You'll be transported back in time to witness the rise of Nazi Germany, the fierce fighting that took place across Europe and Asia, and the eventual defeat of the Axis powers. Whether you're a seasoned history buff or simply looking to expand your knowledge of this pivotal moment in human history, this book is the perfect choice.

Once again, thank you for your choice to purchase this book. I hope you gain a deeper understanding of the Second World War and its lasting impact on the world.

ROOTS OF THE WAR

CHAPTER I: THE AFTERMATH OF WWI IN EUROPE

1918 marked the official end of the First World War. Europe as a whole exhaled a sigh of relief, although the effects of the war would linger for many years to come. The death and destruction that had taken place meant no nation was left unscathed. This chapter will examine the consequences of World War I on Europe, with a special emphasis on Germany, France, and Britain.

Global history was profoundly altered by the complicated events that followed World War I. Millions of soldiers and civilians had died, and entire cities lay in ruins as a result of the war's devastation of Europe. The extremely harsh conditions placed on Germany and its allies by the Treaty of Versailles, which ended the war, planted the seeds of hatred and rage in many Germans that would eventually spark World War II.

Europe was faced with the enormous task of reconstructing its destroyed businesses and communities in the early years after the war. The continent had lost its resources and human capital due to the conflict, and the resulting economic depression had only made matters worse for her citizens. Due to this, many turned to radical ideas in an effort to seek an answer for their problems.

New technology and weapons that would change the scope of warfare forever were also developed during the First World War. For example, the nature of fighting would change as a result of the creation of the tank and the aeroplane on the battlefield and the skies above respectfully. Chemical weapons were also used regularly in the War, horrifying the world and inspiring their condemnation in the years that followed.

New political movements and ideas first appeared in the years following World War I. The world's first solely socialist state was founded in the Soviet Union as a result of the 1917 Russian Revolution. This gave rise to nationalist movements in areas of the world that had been previously colonised by the major empires of Europe. The conflict had also demonstrated the limitations of conventional diplomacy and laid the pavestones for the League of Nations, the forerunner of the United Nations, to be established.

The leaders of Germany viewed the Treaty of Versailles as a betrayal, sparking the "stab-in-the-back-myth", and an embarrassing defeat for their nation. Germany was subjected to severe reparations, which did little but stoke nationalist feeling and give rise to Adolf Hitler and the Nazi Party. Fascist and authoritarian governments grew stronger across Europe as a result of the political unrest and economic suffering of the post-World War II era. We must examine the Treaty's actual provisions in order to comprehend the impact this agreement had on Germany.

THE TREATY OF VERSAILLES

The formal conclusion of World War I was hailed by the signing of the Treaty of Versailles on June 28, 1919. The treaty was an extremely complicated document that had significant repercussions for Germany, the nation that was held solely responsible for causing the outbreak of war. In addition to massive territorial losses, devastating economic reparations, and stringent military constraints, the treaty placed a number of punitive conditions on Germany.

Article 231 of the Treaty of Versailles, which gave Germany and Austria-Hungary sole responsibility for the war, was one of its most significant provisions. The German people despised this paragraph, and referred to it as the "war guilt clause," as they considered it an unfair and unfounded allegation. The clause significantly weakened Germany's sense of national identity and pride by demonising the whole of the German population.

The arts and culture in Germany were significantly impacted by the Treaty of Versailles. Many German intellectuals, artists, and writers believed that the Treaty had deprived Germany of its culture, history and identity. Due to the limitations placed on Germany's military as well as the loss of resources and territory, there was a sense of isolation in Europe.

The German educational system was also significantly impacted by the Treaty of Versailles. The Treaty required that pacifism and internationalism be promoted in the German educational system. As a result, the curriculum was changed to emphasise human rights and peace education and to be more liberal and democratic. In order to depart from the conventional authoritarian and military ideas that were prominent in pre-war Germany, the educational system underwent a change.

The Treaty of Versailles also had a big influence on German nationalism. Many Germans believed that their country had been treated unfairly, and the severe conditions of the Treaty exacerbated their rage and hatred. Germany experienced a rise in nationalism as a result, which was supported by right-wing political parties and radical organisations.

Economically, The Treaty of Versailles devastated Germany. One of the most important provisions of the treaty called for Germany to make up for the losses and damages it caused to the Allies during World War One. Together with other articles, this one severely punished Germany economically, which led to a decade of unrest and poverty.

The German economy was significantly impacted by the reparation payments that Germany was forced to make in accordance with the Treaty of Versailles. The pact left it up to a reparations commission to calculate the whole sum owing; however, the precise amount of the damages was not defined.

The final payment decided upon by the Commission was 132 billion gold marks ($529,411,173,184.36 in today's value circa. 2023), an astounding amount that Germany was unable to pay.

The first payment was due in 1921, and the reparations were to be paid over a period of 42 years. Germany was unable to make the needed payments, and this resulted in a spiral of hyperinflation that utterly destroyed the German economy. Their money became worthless, and the cost of goods and services surged astronomically. The German economy was severely damaged by this hyperinflation, which caused many people to lose their life savings and businesses to fail.

Further, the Treaty included provisions that required Germany to disarm, with the goal of preventing the country from becoming a military threat again. The disarmament provisions had a significant economic impact on Germany as a nation.

Article 159, which required Germany to reduce its military forces to an extremely diminished level, was one of the treaty's most important provisions. Due to the overwhelming number of Germans engaged in the military or sectors associated with the military, this reduction in military forces had an astronomical effect on the German economy.

The decrease in military spending also had an impact on other sectors of the economy, since many companies that depended on military contracts were forced to simply fire the majority of employees or file for bankruptcy altogether.

Furthermore, the Treaty of Versailles strictly prohibited Germany from manufacturing any military hardware. Germany's manufacturing sector, which had previously been almost solely dependent on the production of weapons and ammunition, was significantly impacted by this prohibition on the production of weapons. Due to the restriction, several factories had no option but to shut down, which resulted in further unemployment.

The area and resources that Germany was forced to give up had a significant economic impact as well. Germany was forced to hand over key territory with massive industrial output to a number of its neighbours, including Poland and France. Germany's access to natural resources, such as coal mines and industrial facilities, was hampered by this territorial loss. Her economy was significantly impacted by this resource loss, which resulted in a decline in industrial output and an increase in unemployment.

The political and social fabric of Germany, as well as the stability of its government and its international ties, were significantly impacted by these geographical losses.

The loss of German territory to neighbouring nations was one of the Treaty of Versailles' most significant territorial effects. The pact required Germany to hand over sections of Posen, West Prussia and Upper Silesia to Poland, as well as Alsace-Lorraine to France. Germany's national pride and sense of identity were severely damaged by this territorial loss, which added to the peoples' feelings of animosity and hostility towards the Allies.

The treaty also required that the Rhineland, a significant industrial and economic region of Germany, be demilitarised. As a crucial industrial and transportation hub, the Rhineland's loss of control had a significant effect on Germany's economy. Feelings of vulnerability and insecurity were also exacerbated by the loss of the Rhineland because it exposed Germany to possible attacks from its neighbours.

The German overseas colonies, which were a significant source of resources and raw materials for Germany's economy, had to be dissolved as part of the Treaty of Versailles. Germany's economy was further hurt by the loss of these colonies, making it more dependent on imports from other nations.

The severity of these punishments had a significant impact on the nation's social structure, the welfare of its people, the continuity of its government, and the emergence of extremist political ideologies.

The humiliation and shame that many Germans experienced as a result of the Treaty of Versailles was one of its most significant social effects. The treaty required Germany to accept responsibility for the war's damage and placed full blame for the conflict squarely on Germany and its allies. Many Germans experienced a profound psychological impact as a result of this sense of national shame, which contributed to their feelings of resentment and anger towards the Allies.

The Treaty of Versailles' financial reparations that Germany was required to pay also had a significant social impact. a lot of people lost their life savings, and businesses failed. The economic hardship brought on by the reparations exacerbated social unrest by causing widespread poverty and unemployment.

The Treaty of Versailles also had a significant social impact due to the territorial losses that Germany was forced to accept. As they were compelled to cede land and resources to neighbouring nations, many Germans experienced feelings of betrayal and loss.

This loss of territory also fuelled nationalist sentiment among many Germans and feelings of resentment towards the Allied Powers.

The stability of the German government was significantly impacted by the Treaty of Versailles as well. Germany was required by the treaty to accept democracy and to write a new constitution that upheld fundamental human rights. Although these rules were meant to encourage stability, they also posed tough problems for the new administration. The Nazi Party, which eventually took power in 1933, and other extreme political organisations were difficult for the democratic government to keep under control.

CHAPTER II: THE RISE OF TOTALITARIANISM

Following discussions of the Treaty of Versailles' issues, the harsh punishments imposed, i.e., significant reparations and territorial losses, made the German people feel degraded and extremely resentful of the Allies. Totalitarianism in Germany rose tenfold as a result of the rise of extremist ideologies in this climate of uncertainty.

GERMANY

The Spartacist Uprising of January 1919 was one of this trend's earliest examples. The newly formed Weimar Republic, which had been established following the war, was the target of this communist-led uprising. Although the uprising was quickly put down by the limited army, it served as the catalyst for a number of political and social upheavals that would define Germany's following ten years.

Extremist political organisations started to gain popularity in this environment. The National Socialist German Workers' Party (NSDAP), headed by Adolf Hitler, was the most well-known of these. The NSDAP, or Nazi party, was established in 1920 and quickly gained popularity by appealing to anti-Semitism and German nationalism. Jewish people, according to the propaganda of the party, were to blame for Germany's woes, including the nation's economic woes and wartime defeat.

The NSDAP grew in popularity throughout the 1920s, especially among the working class and in rural areas. The party used paramilitary organisations like the Sturmabteilung (SA) to disrupt opposition meetings and rallies as well as the violent intimidation of its opponents.

Hitler attempted to overthrow the Bavarian government in 1923 during the so-called Beer Hall Putsch, a failed uprising. Despite the coup's failure, it brought Hitler and the NSDAP to the public's attention and boosted their popularity.

Hitler and the NSDAP gained support despite the setback throughout the 1920s. With seats in the Reichstag, the party was the second-largest political force in Germany by 1930. (parliament). The Great Depression and the demise of traditional political parties in the years that followed created an environment of political and economic instability, which only served to increase the party's popularity.

The Weimar Republic's failure to effectively address the nation's issues ultimately aided the Nazi Party's ascent to power. A general feeling of disappointment and rage among the German people was caused, in particular, by the government's failure to stabilise the economy and restore trust in German institutions. Extremist political ideologies, like Nazism, flourished as a result of this providing a favourable environment.

ITALY

Simultaneously, Italy was going through its own development of fascist and totalitarian ideologies as a result of the effects of the First World War.

Both socially and economically, World War One had a profound effect on Italy. In an effort to expand its presence and prominence in Europe, the nation had joined the Allies in their war effort in 1915. However, after failing to achieve its aims, Italy found itself in a chaotic state as a result of the war, with high levels of inflation, unemployment, and political unrest. The ideology of fascism, in this climate, was born.

The Italian Combat Squad, more commonly known as the Fasci Italiani di Combattimento, was established in 1918 by journalist and former socialist Benito Mussolini. The group was made up of a mixture of the young and war veterans who felt a shared hatred for the state of post war Italy. Mussolini's group was minuscule and inconsequential at first, but gained strength as the government fought to solve the nation's issues.

One of the key factors that contributed to the rise of fascism in Italy was the weakness of the existing political parties. The socialist and liberal parties had seen a plummet in their support for their pro war stance, this meant that the country was hungry for a new political movement.

Mussolini and his loyal followers capitalised on this moment, presenting themselves as a radical alternative to the norm in the Italian political landscape.

Early on in the fascist movement, Mussolini was extremely successful in winning over a variety of Italians. He pledged to all of Italy to bring back stability and order, and put a stop to all political corruption. He also promised to bring a new sense of Italian identity. He frequently utilised aggressive words in his discourse to stoke the passions of his followers.

The seizure of the city of Fiume in 1919 was one of the major incidents that contributed to the fascist movement gaining popularity. During the war, Fiume, which is now a part of Croatia, was claimed by Italy, but the Allies gave it to Yugoslavia. Italian nationalists took control of the city and established a new state under the leadership of poet Gabriele D'Annunzio. Even though the occupation came to an abrupt end after just a month, it contributed to Italy's movement towards nationalism and strengthened Mussolini's cause.

In 1921, Mussolini and his supporters started to organise themselves into the National Fascist Party. Mussolini led the party in a military-style fashion, with a handful of devoted lieutenants serving as his closest advisors. The party's doctrine was a synthesis of authoritarianism, nationalism, and militarism. It demanded the establishment of a powerful, centralised government to bring Italy's law and order back.

The National Fascist Party's early years were characterised by intimidation and bloodshed. The paramilitary arm of the party, the Blackshirts, frequently targeted Jews and other minorities in street fights with socialist and communist organisations. In order to gain support from conservative Italians, Mussolini and his allies were able to present themselves as the protectors of stability and order.

In 1922, Mussolini and the fascists marched through Rome, urging the king to elect Mussolini as prime minister. Despite the fact that the march was mostly a bluff, it was successful in persuading the monarch that the fascists posed a real threat.

Upon his appointment as prime minister in October 1922, Mussolini immediately began an expansion of his authority.

A number of measures that were intended to establish a centralised, authoritarian state were implemented during Mussolini's early years in office. He established a one-party system, disbanded the opposition parties, and did away with the parliament. In order to stifle regime resistance, he also established the OVRA, a network of secret police.

The cult of personality that formed around Mussolini was one of the primary characteristics of fascist leadership in Italy. He was portrayed as a commanding, charismatic leader who personified Italian principles.

CHAPTER III: THE APPEASEMENT POLICY AND THE OUTBREAK OF WAR

GERMANY

In the years before the Second World War broke out, Britain and France maintained an appeasement policy towards Germany in an effort to prevent conflict and uphold peace in Europe. Yet, as Hitler began to solidify his authority and further his aggressive territorial goals, this strategy ultimately proved a failure.

To prevent another disastrous war like the one that had just ended, the policy of appeasement was created. It was founded on the idea that by granting Hitler's territorial demands, which were seen as legitimate and reasonable, Britain and France could stop him from pursuing military action.

Hitler took office as Germany's chancellor in 1932, and swiftly started to consolidate his authority by mercilessly assassinating his political rivals and installing himself as the nation's unquestioned leader.

After former President Hindenburg's death in 1934, Hitler combined the roles of Chancellor and President - declaring himself "Führer" or dictator.

Initially, Britain and France's reactions to Hitler's ascension to power were a little unassertive. They hoped that by engaging in diplomatic negotiations for future Sovereign disputes, they could arrive at a peaceful resolution that would meet Hitler's demands without resorting to military action. They were extremely eager to avoid a confrontation with Germany. Hitler announced Germany's rearmament in 1935, brazenly flouting the terms of the Treaty of Versailles and undermining the League of Nations' authority in the process. Despite this, neither Britain nor France attempted to stop him; instead, they continued their discussions in an effort to reach a diplomatic resolution.

Britain and France stuck to their appeasement strategy while Hitler consolidated his power and pursued his aggressive territorial aspirations. They believed that by granting Hitler's wishes, they could stop him from mounting an invasion and dragging Europe into yet another bloody conflict.

Hitler gave the order for the German army to enter the Rhineland in 1936, a demilitarised area created by the Treaty of Versailles following the conclusion of the First World War. The action posed a direct challenge to international law and raised concerns that Hitler was getting ready to invade Europe militarily on a large scale.

The two most powerful countries in Europe at the time, Britain and France, were first hesitant to respond to Hitler's aggression. Britain, which was experiencing a severe economic crisis, and France, which was experiencing political instability, were both preoccupied with their own domestic issues and failed to take significant action to halt Hitler's Lebensraum agenda.[1]

Yet as word of Hitler's Rhineland assault spread, there was rising worry that things would get out of hand. Given that the Rhineland was located near to their borders, the French authorities were particularly concerned because they thought Hitler was planning to launch a full-scale military assault on their nation.

---

[1] Lebensraum (living space) - Hitlers policy in Europe to gain what he saw as "rightfully German" territory.

Britain and France tried to defuse the situation by taking a number of actions in reaction to Hitler's hostility. They both strongly denounced the invasion and demanded that Germany quickly withdraw its troops from the Rhineland. They also informed their own military forces in case Hitler decided to invade.

Hitler's invasion of the Rhineland, however, proved to be a turning point in the lead-up to the Second World War despite these precautions. Hitler was encouraged to continue his aggressive territorial goals as it was clear that Britain and France were unwilling to take a firm stance against Germany.

Europe was on the verge of war in 1938 as a result of Hitler's demands for the Sudetenland, a Czechoslovakian territory with a significant German-speaking population. Hitler was not amenable to negotiations for a peaceful resolution, despite Britain and France's continued commitment to their appeasement strategy.

He gave the German army orders to invade the Sudetenland in September of that year, forcing Britain and France to back down and sign the Munich Agreement, essentially ceding the Sudetenland to Germany.

Many people believed that the Munich Agreement had successfully avoided a devastating war, and it was widely regarded as such. In actuality, Neville Chamberlain, the then-prime minister of Britain, is credited with saying, "I hold in my hand peace in our time," while returning to London after the meeting and holding up the conference treaty.

Hitler, however, immediately made it apparent that he had no interest in living peacefully next to his neighbours. He gave the German troops the order to conquer the remainder of Czechoslovakia in March 1939, essentially annexing it and removing yet another potential barrier to his territorial objectives.

By this time, it was obvious that Hitler could not be placated and that his goals went beyond merely acquiring new territory. It was becoming increasingly obvious that war was unavoidable as a result of his aggressive expansionist plans, which jeopardised the peace in Europe and the rest of the world.

ITALY

Benito Mussolini had kept a careful eye on Adolf Hitler's ascent to power in Germany in 1933. Hitler and Mussolini shared the same ideologies of fascism, nationalism, and militarism. After growing close, the two leaders agreed to the Pact of Steel in May 1939, a military pact that would unite Italy and Germany in the run-up to World War II.

Years of military and diplomatic cooperation between Italy and Germany culminated in the Pact of Steel. Hitler's audacity and success in re-establishing Germany's military and economy following the devastation of World War I had impressed Mussolini. Mussolini viewed the alliance with Germany as a means of enhancing Italy's power and prestige in Europe and posing a threat to France and Britain's hegemony.

Hitler, who had been attempting to assemble an alliance of fascist regimes in Europe, considered the signing of the Pact of Steel to be a tremendous victory. He had a strong ally in the Mediterranean with Italy on board, and he knew that Italian troops would back German military activities. Hitler felt secure because of the alliance because he knew that Italy would not turn against him in the case of a war.

Military cooperation wasn't the only aspect of the Pact of Steel. Additionally, it was a political and intellectual compromise that solidified Mussolini and Hitler's alliance and their shared outlook on Europe. The two leaders viewed themselves as revolutionaries in charge of a new movement that would overthrow the existing system and usher in a new age of grandeur for the country.

Mussolini had already been bringing Italy closer to Germany in the years before the pact. In order to stop the spread of communism in Western Europe, he joined Germany and Japan in signing the Anti-Comintern Pact in 1936.

A crucial test of the fascist regimes' capacity to project their military might had been the Spanish Civil War, where he had also dispatched Italian troops to aid Franco's forces.

Mussolini had already been bringing Italy closer to Germany in the years before the pact. In order to stop the development of communism, he joined Germany and Japan in signing the Anti-Comintern Pact in 1936. A crucial test of the fascist regimes' capacity to project their military might had been the Spanish Civil War, where he had also dispatched Italian troops to aid Franco's forces.

But there were difficulties in the Italian-German partnership as well. Mussolini was anxious that Italy would be left out of Hitler's plans for Europe since Italy had objectives of its own in the Mediterranean and North Africa. Mussolini also had to deal with his own fascist party's rising influence, which was promoting more radical policies and a confrontational posture towards Italy's adversaries.

In spite of these difficulties, Hitler and Mussolini remained close partners in the years preceding World War II. Their camaraderie and their common vision for Europe were powerfully symbolised by the Pact of Steel, which also served as a prelude to the conflict that would soon overwhelm the continent.

POLAND

Adolf Hitler began the Second World War on September 1, 1939, when he launched a full-scale military invasion of Poland. The action, which posed a clear challenge to the authority of the international community, was swiftly denounced by the major European nations, including Britain and France.

Hitler's aggressiveness towards Poland proved to be a step too far, and on September 3, 1939, Britain and France declared war on Germany. The two countries saw Hitler's invasion as an obvious violation of international law since they had vowed to protect Poland's sovereignty and territorial integrity.

Britain and France took some time to respond. Intense discussions took place between the major countries in the days preceding the declaration of war in an effort to find a peaceful solution to the problem. Hitler, however, was adamant about carrying out his objectives of expansion and would not yield.

The British and French armies mobilised and prepared for war fast, but they encountered severe difficulties in the initial stages of the fight. Blitzkrieg, a revolutionary style of warfare invented by the German army, combined air support with quick-moving tanks to devastating effect. The rapidity and severity of the German attack caught the British and French off guard, making it difficult for them to build a successful defence.

The world watched in horror as German soldiers rushed across Poland, bringing death and ruin in their path. Poland fell quickly and brutally. The invasion of Poland signalled the start of a protracted and bloody conflict that would result in the destruction of entire towns and cities and the loss of millions of lives.

Germany, together with Italy, Japan, and newly formed German territories in former Czechoslovakia and Austria, confronted the British Empire and France in their struggle for control in Europe and the rest of the world after the invasion.

Europe was now at war.

CHAPTER IV: TROUBLE IN THE EAST

We may now focus on the Asian Peninsula and the relevance of pre-World War II conflicts there that resulted in Japan's involvement in the fight and ultimately the war against the USA.

As a result of China and Japan's disagreements, tensions in the East were growing following World War One. The region's British and American interests added to the complexity, and there was a high likelihood of violence.

One of the major problems with the Treaty of Versailles is that it stipulated the loss of Germany's colonies abroad without any meaningful plan for re-establishing them under the control of another colonial authority or nation state. As a result, Japan sought to establish itself as the dominating regional power in East Asia. Years of civil strife and international involvement had left the Chinese government defenceless.

The notorious Twenty-One Demands, which would have given Japan enormous economic and political control over China, were made by Japan in 1915 and offered to China. The demands were a result of Japan's goal to expand its influence over China and become the leading nation in East Asia.

The Chinese government was given just two weeks to agree to the Twenty-One Demands when they were presented to them as an ultimatum. Among the demands were clauses that would allow Japan to lease a portion of China's land, seize control of its railroads, and post Japanese advisers in important positions inside the Chinese administration.

In addition, China had to accord Japan preferential status in trade negotiations, allow Japanese nationals unrestricted entry and employment in China, and permit Japan to construct factories and other industrial infrastructure there.

The prospect of Japanese military intervention eventually persuaded the Chinese leadership to accede to the requests after some initial reluctance. All but the criteria that would have given Japan direct influence over China's government were finally met by the Chinese government.

China's independence and sovereignty suffered a serious setback with the acceptance of the Twenty-One Demands. The presence of foreign nations in the area, especially Britain and the United States, made the situation even more difficult. With its colonial holdings in Hong Kong and the New Territories, Britain had long maintained a significant presence in China. The Open Door Policy of the United States, which had been involved in China since the late 19th century, aimed to ensure that all foreign powers had equal access to Chinese markets.

While the United States and Britain both had a stake in the region's stability, their interests also clashed. Britain, for instance, was wary of taking moves that may enrage Japan because it viewed Japan as a crucial ally against Russia. The United States, on the other hand, was suspicious of Japan's expansionist aspirations and had a strong anti-imperialist position.

Britain and the United States both attempted to mediate between the two powers as tensions between China and Japan grew. For instance, the Washington Naval Conference in 1921–1922 aimed to stop the global superpowers' naval weapons competition. Representatives from the United States, Britain, Japan, France, Italy, and a number of other nations attended the conference in Washington, D.C.

The principal goal of the conference, which was presided over by American Secretary of State Charles Evans Hughes, was to set restrictions on the size and power of the world's warships. The Washington Naval Treaty that resulted in these accords set rigid restrictions on the number and size of capital ships that any nation could own.

The treaty also established limits on the size of the other types of ships, such as cruisers and destroyers, and included provisions for the scrapping of older ships.

In addition, the treaty included a number of other agreements, such as a pledge to respect the territorial integrity of China and to maintain open door trade policies in the region.

Initially, the Washington Naval Conference was a major diplomatic success, and it helped to reduce tensions between the major powers of the world. It also helped to establish the United States as a major diplomatic power and laid the foundation for future international agreements.

The conference was a success, but it didn't last long because tensions between Japan and the US remained high in the years that followed. In 1934, Japan finally backed out of the treaty and started expanding its navy once more, paving the way for a new Pacific war.

On September 18, 1931, Japan executed a false flag attack on China by blowing up a section of Japanese owned railway in Manchuria, China. As part of a deal with China, the Japanese military, which had been stationed in the area, blamed Chinese rebels for the attack and used it as a justification for launching a full-scale invasion.

Within a few days, Japanese forces had established a puppet administration that was obedient to Japan and had taken control of Manchuria's major cities and infrastructure. Due to internal conflicts and corruption, the Chinese government was unable to put up a strong fight, and the international community was slow to act.

The effects of the Japanese invasion of Manchuria on the area and the rest of the world were extensive. It signalled a significant uptick in the tensions between China and Japan, and it paved the way for more future Japanese aggressiveness. Additionally, it had important political and economic repercussions since Japan began to assert its power throughout Asia and took control of vital infrastructure and resources in Manchuria.

As a result of Japan's withdrawal from the League of Nations as a result of the Manchuria invasion, she was forced to form alliances with other withdrawing states such as Germany and Italy.

JAPANESE RELATIONS WITH EUROPE

A shared feeling of nationalism and anti-colonialism was at the core of Japan's connection with the Axis powers. Japan considered the Axis powers as potential allies in its fight against Western imperialism and saw itself as an advocate for Asian independence. Fascist philosophy, which promoted strong leadership, national unity, and aggressive expansionism, was popular at the period in Germany and Italy and attracted Japan as well.

The Anti-Comintern Pact, which was aimed at the Soviet Union and its communist supporters, was signed by Japan and Germany in 1936. The agreement cleared the door for future military and economic collaboration between Japan and Germany that indicated a strengthening of their relationship.

Italy and Japan's connection was more nuanced. The two nations battled for influence in Asia and the Pacific even though they held similar anti-colonial and nationalist views. Italy was in confrontation with Japan's territorial aspirations in the region because it had built colonies in East Africa and wanted to increase its influence in Southeast Asia.

Despite these conflicts, Japan, Italy, and Germany all agreed to the Tripartite Pact in 1940, creating a formal military alliance between the three nations. The agreement opened the ground for Japan's entry into World War II and was designed to forge a unified front against the Western world.

A complex mix of components, including political ideology, economic interests, and geopolitical considerations, influenced Japan's relations with the Axis nations. While Japan and the Axis nations shared many of the same ideals and aspirations as Germany and Italy, it was also defined by conflicting interests and rivalries.

JAPANESE INVASION OF CHINA

The full-scale invasion of China by Japan, using their already-established base of operations in Manchuria, was their penultimate offensive before entering the Second World War.

On July 7, 1937, a small skirmish between Chinese and Japanese troops near the Marco Polo Bridge in Beijing swiftly turned into a large-scale conflict, signalling the start of the Japanese invasion of China. Japanese soldiers entered northern China with rapid speed, and by the end of the year, they had seized control of Nanjing.

Infamously known as the "Rape of Nanjing," the Japanese occupation was exceptionally barbaric. Up to 300,000 Chinese soldiers and civilians may have been killed by Japanese soldiers who indulged in rampant rape, murder, and pillage. The atrocities carried out by Japanese forces in Nanjing and other areas of China would have a long-lasting effect on Chinese-Japanese relations and would fuel the rising anti-Japanese sentiment in China that endures to this day.

Chiang Kai-shek, the head of the Nationalist Party, spearheaded the Chinese fight against the Japanese invasion. However, the Chinese soldiers were ill-equipped and disorganised, and the better-trained and better-equipped Japanese forces swiftly outnumbered them.

Internal strife and disagreements within the Chinese resistance were also a hindrance, which allowed the Japanese to advance significantly in the early stages of the struggle.

Millions of Chinese troops and civilians died as a result of the Japanese invasion of China, which ultimately lasted eight years. The Japanese military's deployment of chemical weapons during the battle was another significant event that caused widespread slaughter and devastation. The invasion would have a significant effect on the area and the entire world, adding to the rising hostilities between Japan and the Western superpowers.

With Japan, Germany and Italy united ideologically by 1939, the stage was set for the deadliest conflict in human history.

THE WAR IN EUROPE

CHAPTER V: THE PHONEY WAR

Following the outbreak of the Second World War, which saw Britain and France declare war on Germany as a result of its invasion of Poland, Europe experienced a period of unsettling calm for several months. The Phoney War is the name given to this time period.

On September 3, 1939, the day when France and Great Britain declared war on Germany, the Phoney War officially began. The early months of the conflict saw little real fighting, despite the declarations of war. The French and British armies were waiting for the German army to initiate an all-out invasion of Europe because it had not yet done so.

The British and French recruited their forces and reinforced their frontiers during the first few weeks of the Phoney War. The Maginot Line, a set of French fortifications along the German border, was built. In the meantime, out of concern for German air strikes, the British started evacuating children and other civilians from large cities.

However, life in Europe mostly carried on much as it had before the war.

Although there was little real combat as the months passed, tensions between the Allies and Germany remained high. The French and British forces were on high alert, expecting a German attack that never materialised while the German army was engaged with its invasion of Poland. The only noteworthy activity during this time was a series of naval engagements in the North Sea, where the British navy defeated the German navy on many occasions.

The Phoney War nevertheless had an impact on the people of Europe, despite the lack of action. Many people were afraid and tense since they didn't know what was ahead. Food and other necessities were in low supply, and big cities like London and Paris were constantly in danger of air assaults.

The French and British armies started preparing for a German invasion as the winter of 1939–1940 drew near. They weren't ready for what was to come, though.

The Allies were unprepared for Germany's surprise invasion of Norway on April 9, 1940. The Phoney War was over, and a major struggle erupted in Europe.

It is easy to write off the Phoney War as a time of passivity and calm when looking back on it. But it was a period of uncertainty and worry for the people of Europe. They were aware that war was imminent, but they were unsure of its exact start date or manner. They continued to wait while hoping for the best but fearing the worst.

The Phoney War ultimately served as a short reprieve from the atrocities of World War II. The inhabitants of Europe braced themselves for the impending storm at this time of preparation and anticipation. Even though it may not have had much historical relevance, the time left a lasting impression on the recollections of those who experienced it.

CHAPTER VI: THE FIRST MAJOR GERMAN OFFENSIVES

Norway was unexpectedly invaded by the German troops in the early hours of April 9, 1940. It was a risky action that caught the Allies by surprise and signalled the start of a new stage in the conflict. The earliest German offensives into Norway had a huge impact on all of Europe, altering both the conflict's path and the distribution of power across the continent.

A crucial element of Germany's wartime plan was the invasion of Norway. Norway's proximity to Great Britain and its access to the North Sea made it militarily significant. In order to strike British shipping and stop the supply line to the Allies, the Germans wanted to take control of Norway's ports and airfields. They also desired to construct a base from which to attack Great Britain directly in the future.

German forces used both land and maritime forces in their intricate invasion of Norway. Along the Norwegian coast, German troops made many landings, including in the significant port of Narvik. As a result of the inadequate preparation and equipment of the Norwegian defences, they first encountered minimal opposition. However, as word of the invasion spread, the Norwegian population came together to defend their nation.

Fighting was severe and brutal throughout Norway. The Norwegian army and navy, as well as the British and French forces sent to help the Norwegians, put up a resolute fight against the Germans. It was difficult for the troops to move about during the conflicts because of the snow and ice, which also exposed them to the elements. The Germans advanced significantly in the early stages of the invasion despite these obstacles.

The German invasion of Norway had significant consequences. It served as a wake-up call for the Allies and the beginning of a new stage in the conflict. It demonstrated that the Germans were prepared to take big chances, conduct surprise strikes, and work efficiently in challenging environments.

German aircraft were instrumental in striking Norwegian and Allied forces throughout the invasion, underscoring the significance of air power.

Additionally, the invasion of Norway had wider effects on the distribution of power in Europe. With the fall of Norway, the Germans took control of a vital strategic area and opened a new front in the conflict. They also showed the Allies how they could strike at will and take over territory in unexpected ways. This damaged the Allies' morale and gave the Germans a psychological edge.

The invasion of Norway also had political implications. Neville Chamberlain, the prime minister of Great Britain, was compelled to resign as a result, and Winston Churchill took his place. The British people were motivated by Churchill, a strong and determined leader, to continue fighting despite the setbacks of war.

FALL OF FRANCE

Hitler sought to increase his control over Western Europe after his quick invasion of Norway. France was the major target for the Nazis since it was still far from prepared for full-scale combat with the Germans.

On May 10, 1940, a surprise German offensive through the Ardennes Forest in eastern Belgium signalled the start of the German invasion of France. Military planners had regarded the Ardennes, a densely forested area, as impassable. The heavily guarded Maginot Line that France had constructed along its border with Germany, however, was to be avoided thanks to a strategy the Germans had devised to invade via the Ardennes.

The French and their allies were unprepared for the German invasion across the Ardennes. In anticipation of any German invasion, the French had positioned their strongest troops and most sophisticated weapons along the Maginot Line. But the Germans had created a fresh strategy known as the "Blitzkrieg," or lightning war. The Blitzkrieg employed lightning-quick manoeuvres and coordinated assaults to dislodge enemy defences and swiftly seize vital targets.

The German attack through the Ardennes was a stunning success. They advanced quickly, taking the French defenders by surprise and rapidly moving westward.

The French and their allies attempted to mount a counterattack, but the Germans were too fast and too well-coordinated. They broke through the French lines and continued their advance towards the English Channel.

As the Germans advanced, they encountered stiff resistance from the British and French armies. The British had sent troops to aid the French, and they fought fiercely to slow the German advance. The French, for their part, fought bravely but were hampered by poor leadership and outdated tactics. The Germans continued to advance, however, capturing key ports and cities along the way.

On the beaches of Dunkirk, thousands of Allied soldiers found themselves stranded. The men appeared destined to be caught or slaughtered as the Germans closed in from all sides. But a dramatic event followed: Dunkirk's evacuation.

THE EVACUATION OF DUNKIRK

A large-scale operation involving a flotilla of ships and boats from Britain and France was the evacuation of Dunkirk. The ships arrived in Dunkirk's shallow waters, where they loaded soldiers off the beaches and transported them to safety across the English Channel.

The evacuation was a risky and challenging process. The men had to cross the open beaches while under fire as the ships and boats were constantly being attacked by Nazi bombers and artillery. Nonetheless, the evacuation went on despite the risks, with ship after ship coming to pick up soldiers and take them to safety.

An unimaginable feat of organisation and coordination was also accomplished. Several boats and ships were deployed to various parts of the beaches in accordance with a precisely planned and coordinated schedule of events. The men were divided into groups and led to designated embarkation places, where they were put onto ships that were already at the dock.

The evacuation of Dunkirk was a testament to the strength and spirit of the human race. The soldiers who were stranded on the beaches were able to flee and return to their homes to continue fighting. The evacuation had a significant impact on the war as well since it gave the Allies a chance to reorganise and keep up the struggle against the Germans.

The Nazi offensive continued on despite the troops' successful escape from Dunkirk. The Germans began their subsequent onslaught on June 5 with Paris as their intended target. The city served as the country's political and cultural centre, and its conquest would have a terrible psychological impact on the French populace. The Allied forces offered barely scattered opposition as the Germans stormed over the countryside.

The French government was getting ready to evacuate Paris as the German army moved closer. When the military prepared to protect the capital, hundreds of thousands of residents evacuated the city. The French troops made a brave effort in the outskirts of the Capital, but the overwhelming power of the German war machine was too much for them.

As the Germans invaded Paris on June 14th, there was no resistance, and the city was taken. The French people, who had previously held the belief that their nation's capital was unbeatable, were dealt a terrible blow. The end of the first phase of the war and the beginning of the second made the fall of Paris an important turning point in the war.

The Allies would gather in the days and weeks that followed and start mounting a counteroffensive against the Germans. But the fall of Paris served as a sobering reminder of the German war machine's strength and effectiveness, and turning the tide of the conflict would need a concerted effort from the Allies. Both sides were preparing for the next stage of the fight during the time between the evacuation of Dunkirk and the fall of Paris, which was a period of uncertainty and dread.

The German invasion of France served as another example of the Blitzkrieg's effectiveness and the use of new weapons and techniques in contemporary conflict. The Germans had effectively utilised new strategies and weapons, depending on air support, armoured vehicles, and coordinated assaults to completely overwhelm their adversaries. The French and their allies, on the other hand, continued to use outdated strategies and equipment from World War I.

CHAPTER VII: THE BATTLE OF BRITAIN

Adolf Hitler was on the verge of achieving his vision of the German Reich ruling Europe in the summer of 1940. Hitler focused his attention on Britain, the last stronghold of opposition to his brutal regime, after he had gained control of most of Europe. But he knew he had to deal a crushing blow to Britain's defences before he could begin his planned invasion. He then began what is known as the Battle of Britain, an air campaign against Britain, his final opposition in Western Europe.

Hitler started this campaign for a number of reasons. First and foremost, he was aware that any potential invasion would be seriously threatened by the Royal Air Force (RAF) of Great Britain. Hitler was aware that any chance of an invasion succeeding depended on seizing control of the skies over Britain, which was home to one of the best air forces in the world. Additionally, he thought that by bombing British cities, he could undermine morale among the populace and pressure Britain into capitulating.

net agreed that a full-scale land invasion of the
was required, but only when the weather was
ive to crossing the English Channel. Due to the
eas and lack of rearmament, it was also
owledged that the summer of 1940 represented the
realistic opportunity for an invasion of Britain.

eration Sea Lion, Hitler's codename for his invasion
an against Britain, was a bold and ambitious one. The
erman army was to land on the English south coast,
quickly seize London, and then force the British to
submit. However, in order for the invasion to be
successful, the Germans had to defeat the Royal Air Force
in order to gain aerial dominance over Britain.

In July 1940, the Battle of Britain, a German air offensive, began. The goal of the campaign was to devastate the RAF and prepare the ground for the invasion. Massive bombing raids were conducted by the Germans on British cities, ports, and airfields in an effort to devastate RAF facilities and lower the morale of the British populace.

Fighting was brutal and fierce. German and British aircraft were engaged in dogfights high above the countryside, filling the skies over Britain with the roar of their engines. The two most recognisable aircraft of the war, the Spitfire and Hurricane, were flown by British pilots, who out flew their German adversaries by employing every manoeuvre in the book.

Radar was another covert weapon used by the RAF. The British were able to identify approaching enemy aircraft before they were visible to the unaided eye thanks to their highly developed radar system. Because they could intercept the Germans before they could launch their attacks, this gave the British pilots a crucial advantage.

The campaign also featured a struggle of wills. Hitler anticipated that once the British realised they were up against overwhelming odds, they would quickly submit. However, the British populace resisted giving in. They dug in and fought back, not allowing the German assault to intimidate them.

The fighting was intense, and both sides suffered horrifying losses. Despite being outnumbered and outgunned, the RAF pilots resisted giving up. They operated their aircraft to the point of exhaustion, occasionally losing fuel in mid-air and crashing into the water. However, they persisted in their fight and were able to repel the Germans long enough for them to retreat.

The Battle of Britain marked a turning point in the conflict. Britain was spared from invasion as a result of the German air campaign against it. It was the RAF that prevailed, and this victory had important ramifications.

The victory boosted morale in Britain as the prospect of an invasion hung over it. The triumph demonstrated to the British people that their nation should not be taken lightly and that they were capable of fending off the German war machine.

The victory had important ramifications for all of Europe. The war's trajectory would have been very different if Britain had lost.

Both a key operational base and a significant industrial power would have been lost to the Axis. The outcome may have been very different, and the war may have lasted much longer.

HITLER'S REACTION

Hitler's plans for conquering Europe suffered a devastating defeat in the Battle of Britain. The Führer was incensed because the German war machine had just suffered its first significant setback. Hitler had anticipated that the Luftwaffe would defeat the RAF with ease and decisiveness, opening the door for a ground invasion of Britain. His ego and his dream of a Nazi-run Europe took a serious hit from the failure of this scheme.

Hitler was notorious for his rage and short fuse, so his defeat in Britain set him off in a fury. He vented his anger at his generals and advisers, holding them responsible for the campaign's failure. He contested the RAF's ability to repel the German air force and accused his commanders of being inept and cowardly.

Hitler was adamant that Britain would eventually submit to the might of the German army despite the defeat. He thought that because of their weakness, the British people would be unable to withstand the full force of the Nazi war machine.

Hitler, in a fit of rage, commanded "The Blitz," the air siege of British cities. On September 7th, 1940, the Blitz started, and it lasted for eight months. The German military made a calculated move with the intention of destroying British citizen morale and compelling the government to submit. Although other cities in the nation were also attacked, including Liverpool, Coventry, and Birmingham, London was the primary target.

In the late afternoon of September 7th, London was hit by the first round of bombs. The attack started in East London's docks and industrial districts but quickly spread to other areas of the city. The aircraft of the Luftwaffe flew in waves and dropped high explosive, incendiary, and landmine bombs. As firefighters battled to keep up with the flames, the streets were littered with rubble and debris and fires raged unchecked.

Londoners quickly adapted to living in the middle of a war zone as the bombing continued night after night. While others huddled in basements or under kitchen tables, many people slept in underground stations or air raid shelters. Blackout curtains were required in order to prevent aerial views of the city from being captured, and the government provided gas masks to everyone.

But despite these safeguards, the bombing still caused significant damage. Over a million homes were destroyed and more than 40,000 people were killed during the Blitz. The psychological toll was just as great as people had a hard time adjusting to the ongoing fear and uncertainty.

But despite the destruction, Londoners resisted being broken. Together, they displayed courage and tenacity by volunteering to serve as air raid wardens and firefighters and assisting their neighbours to survive. The Blitz significantly affected how the war played out as well. The German military intended to lower British citizens' spirits, but the opposite occurred.

The bombing brought the nation together and made the military and government more determined to keep up the fight against Nazi Germany.

Hitler, now enraged, was determined to carry out his invasion plans and gave the German army orders to get ready for a major assault on Britain.

Hitler's advisers were more circumspect, though. They urged the Führer to change his mind because they were aware that the German army was not yet prepared for a sizable amphibious operation. They emphasised that an invasion would be risky and expensive and that the British navy remained a powerful force. They also cautioned that the likelihood of other nations supporting the Allies increased the longer the war dragged on.

Deciding to take the advice of his generals, Hitler turned his sites to the East - more specifically - to his allies in the Soviet Union.

CHAPTER VIII: OPERATION BARBAROSSA

With regard to the Soviet Union and its communist ideology, Adolf Hitler had always harboured a deep-seated hatred. He saw the Soviet Union as a vast and untapped source of land, resources, and slave labour and thought that Bolshevism posed a direct threat to the survival of the Aryan race.

Hitler began preparing for a future conflict with the Soviet Union in the years preceding World War II. In August 1939, he and the Soviet Union signed the Molotov-Ribbentrop Pact, which guaranteed that the two countries would not immediately go to war with one another.

The Molotov-Ribbentrop Pact affected Europe significantly. Hitler was able to invade Poland without worrying about the Soviet Union interfering because of a covert protocol that divided Eastern Europe into spheres of influence for the two nations.

Hitler's true motivations for signing the pact were evident. As he dealt with his adversaries in the west, he saw it as a way to protect his eastern front. Hitler was aware that a conflict with the Soviet Union was unavoidable, but he thought the agreement would give him the breathing room and time to get ready. Hitler also saw the agreement as a means of isolating Germany's main enemies at the time, Britain and France.

The choice for Stalin to ratify the Molotov-Ribbentrop Pact was more difficult. Although he was aware that war with Germany was also unavoidable, he thought that forming an alliance with them would give the Soviet Union valuable time to get ready for the fight. Stalin viewed the agreement as a means of seizing control of the Baltic States and a portion of Finland.

Stalin, however, was well aware of Hitler's true motivations. He understood that the agreement was only temporary, and that Hitler would ultimately turn against the Soviet Union. Stalin also understood that the agreement would harm the Soviet Union's standing abroad and make future alliances challenging.

While he dealt with his adversaries in the west, Hitler saw this as a necessary action to secure the eastern front.

Hitler thought that the German army could easily defeat the Soviet Union in a matter of weeks because of its weakness and lack of organisation. Hitler believed his army, which he had spent years preparing and equipping, was the best in the world and would be more than capable of destroying the Soviet Union.

Hitler had a larger vision for the establishment of a vast German empire in Europe and beyond, which included plans for war with the Soviet Union. Since the Soviet Union was the only remaining major power on the continent that could thwart his plans, he thought that it held the key to realising this vision. Due to the Soviet Union's abundant natural resources, such as its oil, gas, and timber reserves, Hitler also considered it a top candidate for expansion.

In order to defeat the Soviet military and seize control of important cities and industrial hubs, Hitler's war strategy against the Soviet Union once again relied on the concept of a lightning-fast invasion (Blitzkrieg).

Hitler intended to quickly overwhelm the Soviet defences and establish a beachhead deep inside the nation using his armoured divisions and air power.

Hitler thought that making a swift and decisive attack would be the key to victory in the war with the Soviet Union. He understood that a protracted war would be disastrous for Germany because of the Soviet Union's enormous population and wealth. Hitler was convinced that the best way to realise his dream of a stronger Germany was with an immediate victory.

But Hitler's plans for a conflict with the Soviet Union were not without difficulties. The country's enormous size and harsh climate presented logistical and strategic challenges. Some of Hitler's military leadership also voiced opposition, arguing that the invasion was hasty and that the German army was not fully ready for such a massive undertaking.

General Franz Halder, the head of the army general staff, was one of the campaign's most prominent critics. Halder had significant concerns with the plan, particularly in light of the considerable distances involved and the enormous manpower and resource reserves of the Soviet Union. Halder argued that the risks outweighed any potential benefits and that the German army was not ready for such a large-scale and long-lasting campaign.

General Erich von Manstein was another well-known opponent of Operation Barbarossa. Manstein thought that attacking the Soviet Union was a mistake. He was regarded as one of Germany's most brilliant military leaders. He argued that rather than risking everything on a campaign in the east, Germany should make securing its western borders and consolidating its victories in Europe its top priority.

Hitler was determined to carry out Operation Barbarossa despite these reservations. He considered the Soviet Union to be an untapped source of valuable resources, including vast reserves of coal and oil. He also thought that Germany's dominance in Europe would be assured by a swift and decisive victory over the Soviet Union.

BARBAROSSA BEGINS

In what would come to be known as Operation Barbarossa, the German army crossed the Soviet border on June 22, 1941, and began the largest invasion in history. With its superior technology and training, the German army initially defeated the Soviet Union with notable success. The invasion was divided into three main thrusts, with the northernmost spearhead aiming to seize Leningrad, the middle spearhead aiming to seize Moscow, and the southern spearhead aiming to seize Kiev and the Caucasus oil fields.

Many Soviet forces were caught off guard and overpowered by the sheer force of the German attack, which allowed the German army to advance quickly. Joseph Stalin was shocked to learn about the invasion.

At first, Hitler's decision to violate their non-aggression pact and attack the Soviet Union had Stalin incredulous. He had faith in Hitler to uphold the terms of the Molotov-Ribbentrop Pact at least for a few more years. Stalin was shocked once he finally realised the circumstances.

Stalin's initial response was to leave his dacha and keep his advisors out of sight. The severity of the situation was something he refused to accept. Stalin was aware that the Soviet Union was woefully unprepared for the invasion. His intelligence agencies had alerted him to the impending attack, but he had discounted the reports as alarmist and exaggerated.

Stalin eventually emerged from his seclusion and started to act. He quickly put together a war council with leading military figures and advisers. Planning to defend the Soviet Union was started after the council discussed the situation. In order to defend against the German advance, Stalin also started to mobilise the military and gave orders for troops to position themselves.

Stalin quickly gathered himself and began to act. He recognised how bad things were and that the Soviet Union was up against a formidable foe. He was determined to defend his nation at all costs, but he was also aware that the Soviet Union had a powerful army and a hardy populace.

Leningrad was the target of the invasion's northernmost spearhead because it was a vital city with significant strategic value for both sides. As the German army advanced quickly towards Leningrad, the sheer size and power of the Soviet defences caught many of them off guard and left them helpless. The city endured great human suffering and death as a result of the German army's siege tactics, but after months of brutal combat, Soviet forces were able to end the siege.

One of the most brutal and destructive sieges of World War II was the Leningrad Blockade, also known as the Siege of Leningrad. Leningrad (now St. Petersburg) was encircled by German and Finnish forces from September 1941 for 872 days, cutting off all supply routes and trapping the city's' over 2 million inhabitants inside.

The situation in Leningrad got worse as winter arrived. All supplies, including those for food and medical care, were cut off to the city. Extreme measures were used by people to survive, such as eating rats, pets, and even wallpaper paste.

Numerous people died from starvation and diseases like typhus and dysentery spread quickly due to a lack of food and water. Over a million people are thought to have perished during the siege, either from starvation, illness, or German bombing.

The people of Leningrad persisted despite the appalling circumstances. They established a network of communal kitchens, rationed the limited food supply, and even started small vegetable gardens inside the city. Several siege-breaking attempts by the Soviet military were also made, but they were largely unsuccessful due to the overwhelming German firepower.

When the Soviet Army finally managed to penetrate the German lines and lift the blockade in January 1944, the siege finally came to an end. The Leningrad population had suffered horribly as a result of the siege, which had lasted more than two years.

The southern front saw some of the bloodiest fighting of the entire war as the German army swept into the Soviet Union.

The Germans wanted to seize control of the region's abundant resources as well as the major cities of Kiev, Odessa, and Sevastopol.

General Gerd von Rundstedt, who oversaw three army groups totalling more than a million soldiers, served as the commander of the German southern spearhead. The Soviet forces met them with fierce resistance, and despite being greatly outnumbered, they fought valiantly and bravely.

The first major battle of the southern campaign was the Battle of Kiev, which began in late July 1941. The Soviet Southwestern Front, with its meagre 34 divisions and 350,000 soldiers, was pitted against the German forces, which had 52 divisions and nearly 700,000 soldiers. The Soviet troops fought valiantly despite their disadvantage, and the conflict continued for more than a month. The city was eventually taken by the Germans, who also captured over 600,000 Soviet prisoners.

The Germans achieved a significant victory with the fall of Kiev because it provided access to Moscow and destroyed a significant Soviet industrial and transportation hub. But it also turned out to be a major setback for the Soviets, who suffered severe losses and lost a significant portion of their army.

The Germans attacked the Crimean Peninsula in August 1941 with the intention of capturing Sevastopol, a significant port city. Despite being greatly outnumbered, the Soviet defenders under the command of General Petrov fought valiantly and held off the German forces for months.

However, the superior firepower of the Germans and the relentless bombardment of the city ultimately led to their victory. In July 1942, Sevastopol fell, costing the Soviet Union close to 100,000 soldiers.

The Battle of Odessa, which started in August 1941, was another event in the southern campaign. General von Manstein's German forces besieged the city for more than two months while pounding the Soviet defenders with artillery and air strikes.

The defenders held out until October 1941 despite being cut off from the rest of the Soviet army, suffering significant losses at the hands of the Germans before finally being forced to submit.

The main German attack moved swiftly in the direction of Moscow, overwhelming many Soviet forces that had been caught off guard. One of the first significant battles of the central spearhead occurred at the Battle of Smolensk, where the German army was able to encircle and decimate a significant portion of the Soviet forces. The battle gave the German army a significant victory and allowed for further advances towards Moscow.

The vast and varied Russian landscape, which included swamps, steppes, and dense forests, was encountered by the German army as it advanced towards Moscow. The Soviet Union's extensive railway network and these natural barriers made it challenging for the German army to maintain supply routes and maintain its momentum.

The central spearhead of Operation Barbarossa underwent a significant turning point at the Battle of Kursk.

Massive offensive operations by the German army were launched against the heavily fortified Kursk salient of the Soviet Union, but the Soviet Union's superior defensive strategies and technological advancements, like the T-34 tank, allowed them to repel the German attack. The German army suffered significant losses in the Battle of Kursk, which was the largest tank battle in history.

During World War II, as the German army advanced into the Soviet Union, Einsatzgruppen, or death squads, accompanied them with the aim of eradicating alleged enemies of the Nazi regime. Hitler's plan to purge Europe of Jews, Communists, and other undesirable groups included the Einsatzgruppen as a crucial component.

Members of the SS, police, and other Nazi organisations made up the Einsatzgruppen. They had the responsibility of lagging behind the German army while rounding up and beheading suspected Third Reich enemies such as Jews, Communists, partisans, and others. Hitler and other influential Nazi party leaders approved of their deeds.

The Baltic states, Ukraine, and Belarus were all occupied territories where the Einsatzgruppen were particularly active. They committed mass murders of Jews and other civilians in these areas, frequently employing mass shootings as their preferred method of execution. To terrorise the local populace and prevent resistance, the killings were frequently done in plain sight.

The brutality and ruthlessness of the Einsatzgruppen were well known. They were notorious for their sadistic behaviour and for enjoying seeing their victims suffer. They were supported by the full weight of the Nazi regime, so they were able to operate with impunity.

The Einsatzgruppen caused conflict within the German army despite their success in carrying out mass killings. Some military leaders were uncomfortable with the death squads' brutality and worried that it would ultimately weaken the war effort. Others, however, believed that the Einsatzgruppen were essential for implementing Hitler's plan for a racially pure Europe.

THE BATTLE FOR MOSCOW

One of the most important and crucial moments of the Second World War was the Battle for Moscow. The battle started when the German Wehrmacht launched a massive assault on the Soviet capital on October 2, 1941. Moscow held a great deal of strategic significance, and its fall would have been disastrous for the Soviet Union.

The German High Command had envisioned a swift victory in the Soviet Union, but by the time the Wehrmacht reached the outskirts of Moscow, the Red Army's tenacious resistance had already slowed the campaign. The German army nevertheless persisted in its advance, and by the end of October they had reached the suburbs.

German strategy called for cutting off the city's supply lines and encircling it from the north and south. The Soviet High Command, on the other hand, had gathered a sizable force of soldiers and weapons to defend the capital. The severe winter, which slowed the German advance and made it challenging for them to maintain their supply lines, helped the Soviet defences.

There was fierce fighting during the Battle for Moscow, and both sides suffered significant losses. The Germans attempted a number of significant offensives, but they were unable to get past the Soviet defences. The Red Army, on the other hand, launched a number of counterattacks that severely damaged the Wehrmacht.

The Battle for Moscow presented a number of difficulties for the German army. They frequently had to operate without enough food, fuel, and ammunition due to the harsh winter's difficulty in maintaining their supply lines. On the other hand, the Red Army was able to make use of the vast resources of the Soviet Union, which allowed them to more easily restock their forces and supplies.

The Germans became worn out and exhausted as the battle dragged on. The soldiers frequently struggled to survive the bitter cold because they were not used to fighting in such harsh winter conditions. Due to the necessity of maintaining a sizable contingent of soldiers on numerous fronts throughout the Soviet Union, the Germans also experienced the issue of overstretching their army.

The German High Command remained adamant about taking Moscow despite these obstacles. However, it became clear as the battle dragged on that they were unable to get past the Soviet defences. The German advance had been effectively stopped by the Red Army, which was now steadily forcing the Wehrmacht back.

The two-month-long Battle for Moscow came to an end on January 7, 1942. The Red Army triumphed, forcing the German forces to flee in defeat. As the first significant defeat for the Wehrmacht in the Soviet Union, the battle had been a turning point in the war.

The outcome of the Battle for Moscow had a significant impact on the remainder of the European War. It had shown that the German army was not unbeatable and that the Red Army was a formidable foe. The Wehrmacht was unable to regain the initiative after their defeat at Moscow, so the battle also signalled the beginning of the end for the German offensive in the Soviet Union.

Both sides had suffered losses in the Battle for Moscow. With over 100,000 soldiers killed or wounded, the Germans had suffered significant losses.

Over 250,000 soldiers had been killed or wounded in the Soviet Union, which had also sustained significant casualties. The Soviet military and civilian populations, however, were encouraged by the victory and had newfound confidence that they could repel the German invaders.

THE SIEGE OF STALINGRAD

The conquest of Stalingrad was one of many strategic objectives that Hitler had during the conflict. Hitler had a number of motivations for taking Stalingrad, and both Germany and Russia greatly valued achieving this goal.

Hitler's desire to conquer Stalingrad was primarily motivated by the strategic value of the city. The Volga River, a significant route for the transportation of goods and resources in the area, ran alongside the city's location. The Germans would be able to better resupply their troops and gain access to essential resources if they were able to take Stalingrad because they would have control over this crucial transportation system.

Stalingrad was a significant industrial hub that produced a variety of goods and materials that were essential to the Soviet war effort in addition to its strategic importance. The Germans could use these industries to aid their own war effort and deny the Soviet Union essential resources if they were able to take Stalingrad.

Hitler was, however, driven to seize Stalingrad for another, more private reason. Hitler and his idea of a Germany that was superior to all others would win a symbolic victory if they were able to take control of the city, which bore the name of the Soviet Union's leader Joseph Stalin. Hitler thought that by taking Stalingrad, he would be dealing a serious blow to the Soviet Union and would go down in history as a great conqueror.

Stalingrad would have been a significant victory for Germany. They would have gained control over an important industrial complex and transportation system, and the Soviet Union's war effort would have suffered significantly. Additionally, it would have provided the German troops, who were struggling to keep up their momentum on the Eastern Front, with a significant morale boost.

Stalingrad had even more significance for Russia, though. The city served as both an industrial and a transportation hub, but it also served as a potent representation of Russian tenacity and resilience. In order to motivate the Soviet people to resist the German invasion, Stalin renamed the city after himself - making it a focal point for the entire country.

The Siege of Stalingrad, which lasted from August 1942 to February 1943, was a conflict between the German Wehrmacht and the Soviet Red Army over control of the vitally important city of Stalingrad.

General Friedrich Paulus's German forces launched a massive assault on the city at the beginning of the conflict, but General Vasily Chuikov's Soviet forces held them off. The conflict quickly turned into a vicious street-by-street brawl in which both sides sustained significant losses.

The Germans considered the conquest of Stalingrad to be an essential step in achieving their ultimate objective of conquistador Moscow and winning the war. However, the Soviet army, which was adamant about preserving the city at all costs, fiercely defended it.

Conditions on both sides of the conflict worsened as it continued. The Soviet army was compelled to fight with dwindling resources and in increasingly harsh weather conditions, while the German army was unable to make any significant gains due to its overworked state and a lack of supplies.

Both sides fought valiantly despite these obstacles, and the battle of Stalingrad quickly rose to the top of the list of the most brutal and devastating engagements of the entire conflict. With hundreds of thousands of casualties on both sides—citizens and soldiers—the city was all but destroyed.

The Soviet army eventually prevailed despite the tremendous losses sustained by both sides, forcing the German army to retreat and effectively ending their hopes of success on the Eastern Front.

The battle of Stalingrad changed the course of the conflict and signalled Nazi Germany's demise.

The battle had enormous significance for Germany. In addition to suffering significant losses in terms of personnel, supplies, and equipment, the Germans' defeat at Stalingrad destroyed the idea that they were invincible and signalled the start of the end for their war effort.

The significance of the battle for Russia was also enormous. The Soviet army faced a long and arduous road to victory after their success at Stalingrad. The Russians saw the defence of Stalingrad as a struggle for their very survival, and it emerged as a potent representation of their tenacity and bravery. The Soviet army turned the tide of the war and eventually drove the Germans back from their borders by holding out against the German assault.

CHAPTER IX: THE GREEK OFFENSIVE

In World War II, a complex web of historical occurrences, political manoeuvring, and strategic considerations preceded the Italian invasion of Greece. Greece, a tiny nation in the southeast of Europe, had long served as a hub for cultures, empires, and wars. Many historical powers sought after it because of its advantageous location in the Balkans with access to the Aegean Sea and the Mediterranean.

Greece endured a period of political unrest and military setbacks in the early 20th century, including the Greco-Turkish War (1919–1922) and the Balkan Wars of 1912–1913. However, the nation started to recover in the 1930s under the direction of Prime Minister Eleftherios Venizelos, who started a number of reforms and modernization initiatives. Despite this, Greece continued to be a small, weak, and isolated country, surrounded by stronger neighbours like Italy, Bulgaria, and Turkey.

The start of World War II in September 1939 presented Greece with new difficulties and perils. The nation proclaimed its neutrality and made efforts to avoid getting involved in the fighting, but because of its location and ties to Britain and France—two of the major Allied powers—it became a potential target for Germany and its Axis allies. Greece was seen as a potential extension of Italy's colonial ambitions in the Balkans and the Mediterranean.

Benito Mussolini, the dictator of Italy, had long fantasised about founding a new Roman Empire and had begun an expansionist policy in both Africa and Europe. He considered Greece to be a weak and defenceless neighbour that Italy could easily subjugate and enslave. Mussolini also hoped to win the respect and allegiance of the Italian people, who were growing weary of his rule and its political and economic shortcomings.

Italy made a number of diplomatic and military moves in the months prior to the invasion to get ready for the assault. Mussolini demanded that Greece hand over a number of important Aegean islands so that Italian forces could occupy them.

When Greece objected, Italy severed diplomatic ties and launched a propaganda offensive to defend its aggression. In addition, Mussolini commanded the sending of substantial forces from Greece across the Adriatic Sea to the Albanian border as well as the beginning of a naval blockade of Greek ports.

Greece, on the other hand, made an effort to stay out of Italy's way and hoped that its neutrality would be upheld. The government reorganised its armed forces and boosted its defences, but it lacked cutting-edge technology and capable management. There was little coordination or cooperation among the various regional commands that made up the Greek army. The country's infrastructure was lacking, with few roads and railroads, and the air force and navy were both small and out of date.

Greece's political climate was also precarious and unstable. The charismatic and well-liked Venizelos, who had retaken control in 1935, was opposed by conservative and pro-German factions. His government was criticised for being corrupt and authoritarian, and his reliance on Britain and France in his foreign policy came under fire.

In addition, social unrest, strikes, and the rise of fascist and communist organisations plagued the nation.

The international community attempted to mediate and avert a war as tensions between Italy and Greece grew. Mussolini rejected the British and French proposals to negotiate a peaceful resolution after guaranteeing Greek independence and sovereignty. Additionally, the Soviet Union, which had a non-aggression agreement with Germany, declared its support for Greece and condemned Italy's aggression.

ITALY INVADES

On October 28th, 1940, the Italian army, led by General Emilio De Bono, launched a surprise attack on Greece, crossing the border with Albania. The invasion marked the beginning of a new phase of the war in the Mediterranean and the Balkans, and it would have far-reaching consequences for the course of the conflict and the fate of the nations involved.

A Greek army of only 140,000 men, the majority of whom were poorly equipped and trained, was pitted against the Italian forces, numbering around 250,000 soldiers and supported by tanks, artillery, and aircraft. The Greeks were nonetheless adamant about defending their country and thwarting Italian aggression.

Greece's initial response to the invasion was prompt and forceful. Under the direction of General Alexandros Papagos, the army launched counterattacks on a number of fronts in an effort to drive the Italians back and seize advantageous positions. The Greeks also had the advantage of fighting in their own mountainous, rough terrain, which limited the manoeuvrability of the Italian tanks and artillery.

At Elaia-Kalamas, one of the invasion's opening significant battles was fought. During World War II, this was a crucial time in the Italian invasion of Greece. The first significant clash between the Italian and Greek armies occurred in November 1940, close to the Greek-Albanian border.

General Emilio De Bono's Italian army crossed the Albanian border a few weeks earlier in an attempt to seize important targets in northern Greece, including the city of Ioannina and the port of Thessaloniki. The Italian forces were well-equipped, well-trained, and nearly two to one more numerous than the Greek army. General Alexandros Papagos oversaw a force of about 140,000 men, the majority of whom were ill-equipped and undertrained.

The Italian army moved closer to Ioannina, which was being defended by the Greek army, signalling the start of the Battle of Elaia-Kalamas. With machine guns, mortars, and anti-tank weapons as reinforcements, the Greeks had set up a formidable defensive line. The area's mountainous and rough terrain made it challenging for the Italian tanks and artillery to manoeuvre.

With the assistance of artillery and aircraft, the Italians launched their initial assault on the Greek positions. The Greeks put up a ferocious fight back and used their weapons to devastating effect. The Greek machine guns and snipers heavily wounded the infantry, and the Italian tanks were unable to breach the Greek defences.

Both sides sustained significant losses during the battle, which lasted for several days. At various points, the Italians were able to breach Greek defences, but they were unable to capitalise on their victories because of logistical issues and opposition from the Greek rear-guard units. On the other hand, the Greeks were regularly able to defend their position and deal a lot of damage to the Italian army.

The Italian army's attempt to cross the Kalamas River, which cut through the battlefield, was one of the battle's pivotal moments. The Greeks had set up defensive positions on the other side of the swift, deep river. The Greek defenders pelted the Italians with machine-gun fire as they attempted to cross the river using pontoons and boats. Numerous Italian soldiers perished in the river or from Greek fire.

A significant victory for the Greek army and a boost to Greek nationalism were achieved at the Battle of Elaia-Kalamas. It demonstrated that the invaders could be driven back and that the Greek army could stand its ground against more powerful adversaries.

The battle also gave the Greek people the will to fight against the Italian occupation and aid in the war effort.

However, the outcome of the invasion did not change as a result of the victory at Elaia-Kalamas. Despite its setbacks, the Italian army continued to advance into Greek territory, seizing a number of towns and villages and severely harming the civilian populace.

Additionally, the Italian invasion of Greece had an impact abroad. Greece's independence was guaranteed by Britain and France, who then declared war on Italy and started sending troops and supplies to the Greeks.

The Greek army launched a counteroffensive against the Italian army in November 1940. The objective of the counteroffensive was to repel the Italian forces and retake any territory that had been lost during the initial stages of the invasion.

The Battle of Pindus in late November was one of the first victories of the Greek counteroffensive.

With the aim of capturing the vital town of Metsovo and securing their flank, the Italian army had advanced into the Pindus Mountains. But the Greeks launched a surprise assault, which caught the Italians off guard. General Konstantinos Davakis' Greek army was able to outmanoeuvre and encircle the Italian forces by taking advantage of the terrain. After suffering significant losses, the Italians were forced to retreat and give up their positions in the mountains.

The Greek army continued its offensive after their victory at Pindus, taking control of several significant towns and passes in northern Greece. The counteroffensive's most important victory was the seizure of Korç and the Klisura Pass in early January 1941. The Klisura Pass, which controlled the route between Albania and western Greece, was a crucial strategic location.

Using mountain troops to scale the sheer cliffs and attack the Italian positions from behind, the Greeks launched a surprise attack on the defenders. Being caught off guard, the Italians were unable to defend their position.

The Italian army was forced to flee after the Greeks defeated them at Klisura Pass, abandoning their positions in Albania and concentrating their forces in Greece.

The Italian army started to struggle due to a shortage of supplies and reinforcements as the Greek counteroffensive gained momentum. Due to inadequate funding for the invasion, the Italian high command had miscalculated the size and tenacity of the Greek army. It was difficult for the Italians to supply and reinforce their troops because of the harsh winter weather and the mountainous terrain.

In spite of these difficulties, the Italian army persisted in repelling the Greek counteroffensive by launching counterattacks and defending crucial positions. However, they lost ground and sustained significant losses as they were progressively driven back towards the Albanian border. The Greek army had reclaimed a large portion of the territory it had lost during the initial invasion by the end of January 1941, and it had also severely damaged the Italian army.

THE GERMAN INTERVENTION

Hitler had no choice but to launch a full-scale invasion of the nation in order to support Mussolini's forces after Italy's failures in Greece. Hitler's plan to secure the Balkans and prepare an attack on the Soviet Union included the invasion, which started in April 1941. General Wilhelm List's German army overran the Greek army as it invaded Greece from Bulgaria and Yugoslavia, forcing the Allied forces to flee to the south and east.

The German army advanced quickly, capturing strategic positions and towns with their superior firepower and strategies. Thermopylae was a strategically important pass that connected central Greece with the south, and it was the site of one of the invasion's earliest significant battles. The Greek army, under the command of General Ioannis Pitsikas, put up a strong fight, taking advantage of the challenging terrain. German forces, on the other hand, were able to flank the Greek positions and drive them back. The German army gained a significant advantage in the Battle of Thermopylae, enabling them to advance deeper into Greece and cut off the Allied forces' supply routes.

The Allied forces were compelled to retreat to the south and east as the German forces advanced. The ANZACs, also known as the British, Australian, and New Zealand soldiers, were evacuated to the island of Crete. In an effort to mount a last-ditch defence against the German air force, the Greek army also withdrew towards the Peloponnese.

However, the German army persisted in its advance, seizing significant towns and cities along the way. After a brief but intense battle on April 27th, the Germans took control of Athens, the capital of Greece. German artillery and bombs severely damaged the city, destroying many of its historic structures and monuments. Additionally, the Germans took control of Corinth, an important port city in the Peloponnese, opening up a supply route to the Greek islands and the North African campaigns.

In May 1941, the German army launched Operation Mercury, a significant airborne invasion of the island of Crete. The goal of the operation was to establish air and naval bases in the eastern Mediterranean while also securing the island.

On May 20th, 1941, a massive assault on the island's airfields and ports signalled the start of the German airborne invasion. Over 22,000 German paratroopers and glider troops were dropped onto the island from the air while troops were landed on the beaches by naval forces.

The British, Australian, New Zealand, and Greek forces that made up the Allied forces put up a valiant fight. The Allied forces fought valiantly and determinedly in spite of being greatly outnumbered and outgunned.

The Allied forces, who fought valiantly to defend the island's strategic positions, put up a strong fight against the Germans. The German troops were able to defend their position in the face of numerous counterattacks from the Allies thanks to excellent air support.

Despite the opposition from the Allies, the German forces eventually took control of the situation. They took control of a number of significant towns and locations, including the Maleme airfield, which allowed them to rule the skies over Crete.

The Germans were able to launch devastating attacks on the Allied positions and continuously support their ground forces thanks to their air superiority.

However, the German victory wasn't without a price. With over 4,000 paratroopers killed and numerous others injured, the airborne invasion had taken a heavy toll on the German forces. Over 4,000 of the Allied forces' casualties were killed or taken prisoner.

A large-scale airborne invasion was used for the first time in history during the battle for Crete. The German victory cut off a crucial Allied supply line and gave the Axis powers control of the eastern Mediterranean.

Both the Allies and the Axis powers felt the effects of the battle strongly. The loss of Crete was a major setback for the Allies because it severed a vital supply line and forced them to rely on farther-flung bases in Egypt and the Middle East. It also highlighted the need for a better-coordinated and more effective defence in the Mediterranean and the weakness of Allied defences there.

The victory at Crete was a significant tactical success for the Axis powers. It gave them a starting point from which to conduct additional operations in the Mediterranean and put British control of the Suez Canal in jeopardy. The Germans pursued additional airborne operations in the area as a result of the airborne invasion's success.

The German invasion of Greece marked the end of the Greek resistance and opened the door for its occupation, which proved to be a crucial turning point in the war. The invasion had broader strategic repercussions as well because it forced the Allies to forego their plans for a front in the Balkans and instead concentrate on defending Egypt and the Middle East.

Greeks suffered greatly during the Italian invasion and the ensuing counteroffensive, so the German invasion of Greece was a devastating blow to them. The Greek people would endure unspeakable hardships and atrocities for the entire four-year duration of the occupation. The Greek resistance would nevertheless keep up its resistance to the occupation, and the world would come to look to them as an example of hope and inspiration.

CHAPTER X: THE NORTH AFRICAN CAMPAIGN

The North Africa Campaign of World War II was a protracted conflict that lasted from 1940 to 1943. It began with the Italian invasion of North Africa in September 1940. The initial Allied response was slow and disorganised, and it was not until the German intervention in early 1941 that the campaign began in earnest.

On September 13, 1940, Italy launched its invasion of North Africa in an effort to increase the size of its colonial holdings there by advancing into Egypt and towards the Suez Canal. The Italian invasion initially caught General Archibald Wavell-led British and Commonwealth forces off guard. They were unprepared to respond because they had not anticipated an attack in North Africa. They were able to mount a defence and drive the Italian forces away, though.

Australia, New Zealand, and South Africa sent troops to support the British and Commonwealth forces. Early on in the campaign, these soldiers—also known as the ANZACs—had a significant impact. They had the training and tools necessary to adapt to the harsh desert conditions.

The Battle of Sidi Barrani, which got under way in December 1940, was the campaign's first significant engagement. Under the direction of General Rodolfo Graziani, the Italian forces moved closer to the fortress at Sidi Barrani that was occupied by the British. But the British and Commonwealth forces, under the command of General Richard O'Connor, met them with a resolute defence. Inflicting significant casualties on the Italian forces and forcing them back towards their own borders, the British forces used their tanks and artillery to devastating effect.

Italian forces regrouped and began a second offensive in January 1941 despite this setback. They moved closer to Tobruk, a port controlled by the British, this time. The Italian attack was, however, once more repelled by the forces of the British and Commonwealth.

The Italian forces suffered significant losses as a result of the British forces' effective use of infantry, artillery, and tanks. The Italian forces were driven back to their starting positions by the time the battle was over, and the British and Commonwealth forces had taken control of Tobruk.

In March 1941, the Italians began a third offensive in response to the British victories. They moved closer to the town of El Agheila this time. The Italian attack caught the British and Commonwealth forces off guard, and they were forced to retreat towards the Egyptian border. The Italian advance, though, moved slowly, allowing the British to regroup and launch a counterattack. Italian forces were successfully surrounded by British and Commonwealth forces, who then dealt them a crushing defeat. The British and Commonwealth forces were able to advance into Libya while the Italian forces sustained significant losses.

There were several tactical mistakes made by the Italian forces during the campaign in North Africa. They frequently took too long to respond to British advances, and they didn't use their tanks and other armoured vehicles to their full potential.

On the other hand, the British and Commonwealth forces were able to utilise their tanks and artillery effectively, and they were able to effectively coordinate their attacks.

With the German intervention, the situation in North Africa underwent a significant change. General Erwin Rommel's German Afrika Korps arrived in North Africa in February 1941. It was clear right away that the Afrika Korps would be a tough opponent due to their superior training and equipment.

Rommel quickly made a name for himself as a capable leader, and he was able to take advantage of the gaps in the Allied defence. He was especially successful at outflanking and encircling Allied positions by using mobile armoured units.

The German army had made significant progress in North Africa by November 1941, seizing the important port of Tobruk and cutting off the Allies' supply routes to Egypt. General Auchinleck's British and Commonwealth forces launched a counteroffensive with the intention of retaking Tobruk.

The German army continued to be in control, and the Allies were unable to make any significant progress.

Between November 1941 and June 1942, there were several seesaw battles during which both sides gained and lost ground. Numerous attacks were launched by the British and Commonwealth forces against the German positions, but they failed to make any real headway. General Rommel was adamant about retaining his gains while the Germans kept fortifying their positions.

The Germans launched a significant offensive against the Allied positions at Gazala in December 1941. Both sides suffered significant losses in the fierce battle, but ultimately the Germans prevailed. As the Germans moved closer to the vital port of Tobruk, the Allies were forced to retreat.

The Germans launched an aggressive assault on the Allied positions as they advanced towards Tobruk in January 1942. Despite putting up a valiant fight, the British and Commonwealth forces were ultimately forced to withdraw, and the Germans took control of Tobruk.

The loss of Tobruk dealt the Allies a heavy blow by cutting off their supply routes to Egypt and giving the Germans a strategic base from which to launch additional assaults.

By May 1942, the Germans had reached the Egyptian border as they had kept up their advance. The British and Commonwealth forces, on the other hand, were not prepared to surrender easily and started preparing for a major offensive. General Montgomery assumed command of the Allied forces in June 1942, and he immediately began preparing his soldiers for the upcoming German offensive.

THE SECOND BATTLE OF EL ALAMEIN

An important battle that lasted from October 23, 1942, until November 4, 1942, was known as the Second Battle of El Alamein. The British forces launched a heavy artillery barrage to start the battle. The bombardment was designed to weaken the German defences and leave openings in their lines of defence. The British forces then launched a massive tank assault, pushing through the openings in the German lines.

The Rommel-led German forces were ready for the British assault. They had dug in far and set up a complex network of defensive positions. The British forces, however, were tenacious and continued to advance, piercing the German defences with the help of their tanks.

Both sides suffered severe losses in the hard-fought battle. But the British forces advanced steadily, inch by inch driving the Germans back. Although the Germans put up a valiant fight, the British attack's relentlessness eventually wore them down.

The use of creative strategies by the British forces was one of the main factors in their victory. The strategy Montgomery had developed called for swarms of tanks to pierce the German defences. The artillery pieces that supported the tanks provided cover fire and weakened the German positions before the tanks moved in.

The artillery fire was timed to advance just in front of the tanks in a strategy known as a "creeping barrage" used by the British forces.

This made it more challenging for the Germans to mount a successful defence because the tanks could advance while the German positions were still being heavily artillery fired upon.

The British forces gained more and more ground as the battle went on. By the time the battle was over, they had forced the Germans back towards the Mediterranean coastline. The British and Commonwealth forces had won the battle, which signalled a turning point in the North African campaign.

The British and Commonwealth forces made significant progress with their victory at the Second Battle of El Alamein. It gave them control of the Suez Canal, a key strategic resource, and it cut off the Axis forces' access to Europe's supply routes. As a result, the Axis forces were depleted, making it more challenging for them to launch successful campaigns in other war zones.

THE TURNING POINT

The campaign's pivotal moment occurred in late 1942, when a string of occasions shifted the tide in the Allies' favour.

Operation Torch, the biggest amphibious invasion to that point in history, was launched by British and American forces at the beginning of November 1942. The mission was to seize French-held North Africa, take over the Mediterranean, and launch a western flank attack on Axis forces.

As a result of the successful landings, the Allied forces quickly took control of Morocco and Algeria, cutting off Rommel's supply routes and forcing him to retreat. The Axis powers had stopped being aggressive as the tide had clearly shifted. In the meantime, Allied forces started to fortify their position in North Africa by increasing their troop and supply levels.

The Axis powers found themselves on the back foot as the Allied forces solidified their gains. Rommel had to flee from Egypt into Libya as his supply lines became more and more exposed. General Bernard Montgomery's British Eighth Army launched a counteroffensive during this time, forcing the Axis forces back even further.

The Axis powers' decision to withdraw was not made hastily. They understood how crucial North Africa was as a supply route for the Mediterranean and the Middle East. However, the North African campaign came to an end with the loss of Tunisia in May 1943, and the Allies had achieved a significant victory.

The Torch landings had a profound effect and marked a turning point in the campaign. The Axis powers were forced to retreat while the Allies were able to establish a foothold in North Africa and build up their forces. The pivotal change in momentum allowed the Allies to seize the initiative and mount effective offensives against the Axis forces.

There were significant repercussions for the rest of the war, particularly in Europe, from the Allied victory in this campaign. The Axis powers' relations underwent a significant change in the wake of the North Africa Campaign, which ultimately led to the Axis powers' ultimate defeat.

The relations between the Axis powers started to deteriorate after their defeat in North Africa. Italy, which had been the main aggressor in North Africa, had experienced a severe loss and was ashamed of the campaign's outcome. Mussolini had now directed two significant offensives that ultimately failed, the first of which was the 1940 invasion of Greece. Hitler had grown wary of Mussolini's ability to lead in international conflict and saw him as a threat to his goal of achieving world dominance.

The Italian people started to doubt the wisdom of their involvement in the war after this defeat, which also resulted in a decline in confidence in Mussolini's leadership at home.

Germany, which had aided Italy in North Africa, also saw a significant decline in the quality of its armed forces. The German military suffered a serious setback as a result of the loss of numerous soldiers, pieces of equipment, and supplies. With the Soviet Union in the east and Allied forces in North Africa, Germany was now engaged in a two-front war as a result of the loss of North Africa.

The war was significantly affected by the Allied victory in North Africa. It was the first time that the Allies had soundly defeated the Axis in a significant theatre of the war, and the Axis powers' defeat in North Africa dealt them a severe morale blow. The victory also illustrated the viability of Allied tactics and strategy and demonstrated their capacity to conduct extensive offensive operations.

Due to their defeat in North Africa, the Axis powers were also forced to spend a significant amount of their wartime resources defending against Allied attacks in the region. The Axis powers' capacity to launch offensive operations elsewhere was hampered by this resource allocation, which ultimately led to their downfall.

Political ramifications of the Allied victory in North Africa were also significant. An important propaganda victory for the Allies was the Axis defeat in North Africa, which increased public support for the war effort. Disagreements between the United States, Great Britain, and the Soviet Union had put strain on the Allies' coalition, which it also helped to strengthen.

CHAPTER XI: THE STATE OF EUROPE 1943

1943 saw Europe as a continent completely destroyed by war. Its cities were filled with the sounds of gunfire and explosions, and the devastation of battle had left the countryside scarred. A large portion of Europe had been taken over by Nazi Germany, which left a path of devastation and suffering in its wake.

However, despite the gloom that dominated the continent, there were also rays of hope. Many nations saw the emergence of resistance movements, which worked tirelessly to topple the Nazi government and open the way for liberation. On the Eastern Front, the Allies had started to gain ground by retaliating against the German advance. And preparations were being made for one of history's boldest and most audacious military campaigns - the D-Day landings.

Europe was a continent that was both known and unknown as it stood on the cusp of a momentous change.

Millions of people had their lives disrupted by the war, forcing them to adjust to new situations and difficulties. Food and other necessities were in short supply, and rationing had become ingrained in society. Civilians had to adapt to living in constant fear of death and destruction due to the threat of bombing raids.

But there were also indications of resiliency and defiance at the same time. People had developed new strategies for helping one another when times were tough and had learned to get by on less. To aid in the war effort, women had taken on new jobs and responsibilities in offices and factories. And all over the continent, there were people who were ready to fight against the Nazi occupation and risk their lives.

The state of Europe in 1943 was a complex and multifaceted picture. It was a continent in turmoil, but it was also a continent that was fighting back. The war had brought out both the best and the worst in people, revealing the depths of human cruelty but also the heights of human courage and compassion.

BRITAIN

The war had already lasted more than three years for Britain, and the country was preparing for the upcoming major offensive. The Allied forces hoped to gain a foothold in France and turn the tide of the war, so preparations for the D Day landings were already under way. But even as the country was getting ready for this critical time, it was also dealing with the fallout from the Blitz, the effects of rationing, and the consequences of Alan Turing's amazing success in breaking the Enigma code.

Britain had experienced the effects of the Blitz both physically and psychologically. Many of the country's cities were destroyed by the Germans' persistent bombing campaign, leaving nothing but rubble and ruins in their wake. But the people had also suffered because they had to put up with months of nightly air raids and constant danger. Despite this, the country was resilient and had a sense of unity and resolve to face the difficulties that lay ahead.

One of the biggest difficulties was rationing. Due to supply chain disruptions caused by the war, it was challenging to import necessities like food and fuel. As a result, the government instituted a system of rationing that restricted the quantity of particular goods that people could buy. People had to find ways to stretch their resources as far as they could and make do with less as a result.

The preparations for the D Day landings were progressing against this backdrop. The operation, which required the coordination of troops, ships, and aircraft from numerous nations, was one of the most intricate and ambitious military operations in history. The operation's success could mean the difference between victory and defeat, so the stakes were very high.

A remarkable intelligence gathering breakthrough was at the core of the planning effort. Enigma was a form of encryption that the German military employed, making it nearly impossible for the Allies to decipher their communications.

However, a team led by mathematician Alan Turing had already cracked the code in 1941, giving the Allies a significant tactical advantage. The Allies were able to foresee German troop movements and plan their own movements in accordance with the intelligence obtained through Enigma, which was crucial in the planning of the D Day landings.

The country readied itself for the next stage of the conflict as the year went on. While the effects of rationing and the Blitz continued to be felt strongly, preparations for the D Day landings went forward as planned. As the country banded together to face hardship, there was also a sense of hope and resolve.

Looking back, it is evident that 1943 was a crucial year in the history of Great Britain. It was a time of extreme hardship and sacrifice, but it was also a time of extraordinary bravery and ingenuity. The nation's commitment to fighting for its freedom and future is best demonstrated by the preparation for the D Day landings. Although the Blitz and rationing had a significant impact, they were unable to break the spirit of a people who refused to accept defeat.

FRANCE

France was a nation that was besieged in 1943. The French people had suffered greatly under the Nazi occupation, with constant reminders of their loss of freedom and autonomy. In Vichy, where they had fled, the French government had installed a collaborationist government that worked with the Nazi occupiers. Others, however, resisted the occupation and put their lives in danger to fight against the Nazi regime.

France had experienced a reign of terror as a result of the Nazi occupation. Those who opposed the occupation were relentlessly pursued by the Gestapo and other Nazi organisations. Nazis frequently used arbitrary detentions, torture, and summary executions to crush any opposition to their rule. The Vichy government, on the other hand, did little to shield the French people from the horrors of the occupation and was an open collaborator with the Nazi regime.

However, there were those who resisted the occupation even in the face of such repression. As a result of their tireless efforts to disrupt German operations and gather information about their activities, the French Resistance had become a crucial force in the fight against the Nazis. The desire to see their country freed from the yoke of Nazi tyranny brought resistance fighters from all walks of life together.

With cells dispersed throughout France, the Resistance operated covertly. To avoid the Nazis' attention, they used a network of safe houses, secret messages, and encrypted communications. From straightforward acts of sabotage to more intricate operations like assassinations and sabotage of German supply lines, resistance fighters engaged in a variety of activities.

The French Resistance persisted in gaining power and influence despite the dangers. By 1943, they had become a significant headache for the Nazi occupiers, causing havoc with their operations and giving the Allies vital intelligence.

Resistance fighters came from all spheres of society, including farmers and intellectuals, and they were brought together by a common desire to see their nation freed from Nazi rule.

However, those opposing the occupation were not just the Resistance. There were also those in France who made the decision to work with the Nazis, either out of fear or because they thought it was the best way to safeguard their own interests. Small-time criminals and wealthy industrialists, who saw an opportunity to make money from the occupation, were among the collaborators.

The introduction of the Service du Travail Obligatoire (STO), which required French citizens to work in German factories, was one of the major events of 1943. Deeply unpopular, the STO sparked widespread strikes and protests across France. With attacks on supply lines and equipment sabotage, resistance fighters also targeted the German factories where French labourers were being forced to work.

The occupation took a terrible toll on the people of France. Food and other necessities were hard to come by, and as people struggled to make ends meet, the black market grew. With the Nazi occupation continuing with no apparent end in sight, a constant threat of violence and repression hung over their heads.

THE SOVIET UNION

The Soviet Union was engaged in a fierce conflict with Nazi Germany in 1943. Soviet citizens had suffered greatly as a result of the war, with millions of lives lost and entire cities reduced to ruins. However, the Soviet people were tenacious and, under Joseph Stalin's direction, they were determined to carry the battle to victory.

The Soviet Union was caught off guard when the Nazis invaded in 1941, and the initial German advances were disastrous. However, the Soviet people had united in defence of their nation, and by 1943, the war's momentum had started to shift. The Soviet military had developed new tactics and strategies to combat the German war machine after learning painful lessons on the battlefield.

The Soviet Union's extensive rearmament programme was one of the most important factors in its ability to fight back against the Germans. Stalin had invested a significant amount of money in strengthening the Soviet military, and by 1943, the Red Army was a powerful fighting force. The Soviet Union was producing tanks, planes, and weapons at a rate never before seen, giving the troops the means to confront the German army.

However, this rearmament came at a high cost in terms of resources and human lives. The war had caused the Soviet people great suffering, with millions of civilians being killed or displaced by the fighting. Cities had been completely destroyed, and the nation's infrastructure had suffered severe damage. But despite these losses, the Soviet people remained determined to fight on.

Stalin, on the other hand, was instrumental in directing the Soviet Union's war effort. He was a brutal leader who demanded complete loyalty from his followers and was not averse to making unpopular choices.

The Soviet Union had adopted a scorched earth policy under Stalin's direction, obliterating resources and infrastructure to keep the advancing German army from accessing them.

Stalin also contributed to the creation of the Soviet Union's propaganda apparatus. The government-run media was employed to sway public opinion and mobilise backing for the war effort. Stalin was portrayed as a hero who triumphed over the fascist invaders with the help of the Soviet people.

The Soviet Union began to attack in 1943. In a series of offensives, the Red Army drove the Germans back and freed areas that had been under Nazi rule for a long time. Despite the extreme hardship the Soviet people had to endure, their tenacity and fortitude had paid off.

GERMANY

Germany's situation was precarious in 1943. For more than ten years, Adolf Hitler had been in charge, and under his direction, Germany had entered a disastrous war on two fronts.

Germans were suffering, and the general public's sentiment was starting to shift against Hitler and his government.

Hitler's cabinet was made up of partisans who shared his commitment to creating a totalitarian government. There were many military leaders in this cabinet who had become powerful during the conflict. They were prepared to make difficult choices in order to accomplish their goal of winning the war at all costs.

Nevertheless, a few members of Hitler's cabinet had grown weary of the way the conflict was going. They understood that the German people were suffering because the war could not be won. Hitler, however, disregarded their counsel and redoubled his determination to wage a total war.

Germany had suffered greatly as a result of the two-front war. The Red Army drove the German army back on the eastern front, reclaiming areas that had been under Nazi rule for years. The Allied forces were advancing steadily in the west, landing in North Africa and Italy and getting ready to launch a major invasion of France.

The effects of the war were starting to be felt by the German people. There was a shortage of food and other resources, and rationing had become commonplace. Hitler and his regime were facing growing public opposition as the propaganda machine lost its power. Even a few small-scale protests and acts of resistance occurred as Germans started to doubt the need for the war.

The relationship between Germany and Italy was also deteriorating. Italy had been a crucial ally of Germany during the war, but the country's military was struggling and the populace was losing faith in their government's willingness to support the Nazis. The performance of the Italian military was coming under increasing fire from Hitler, and tensions between the two countries were starting to rise.

Hitler's management style was becoming more unpredictable. He was prone to outbursts of rage and frequently refused to take his subordinates' counsel. He was obsessed with preserving his ideal of a totalitarian state and would do anything to make it happen.

ITALY

Italy was experiencing a crisis unlike any other at the start of the year. While actively participating in World War II and fighting alongside Germany and Japan, the nation found that things were not going well. Many Italians believed their nation was fighting a losing battle, which divided public opinion on the war.

Benito Mussolini, the president of the nation, was at the centre of the crisis. Since taking office in 1922, the fascist dictator had changed Italy in a number of important ways. Through a number of public works initiatives, he had improved the educational system, made the trains run on time, and produced jobs. But his actions had also resulted in a significant transfer of power into his own hands, and over time, he had grown more and more authoritarian.

Numerous Italians were alarmed by Mussolini's friendship with Hitler. Both Mussolini and Hitler were fascists, but they had different ideas about how Europe should develop.

Hitler viewed Italy as a junior partner in a German-dominated Europe, whereas Mussolini saw it as a great power that could stand on its own. In spite of these differences, Mussolini had sided with Hitler, and Italy had agreed to fight in the war.

Italy's military fortunes continued to deteriorate throughout 1943. After a string of humiliating losses in North Africa, the country had suffered, and the Allies were now getting ready to invade Italy. Numerous Italians started to question whether Mussolini's alliance with Hitler was a mistake. There was little that can be done to avert an invasion that is now a very real possibility for the nation.

Mussolini's standing in society was deteriorating, and there were growing demands for his ouster. Mussolini, however, remained resolute and steadfast in his refusal to resign. He persisted in motivating his followers and continued to make fiery speeches in which he vowed to lead Italy to victory.

Mussolini started to lose control of the situation as the year came to a close. Italy was clearly going to lose when the Allies invaded Sicily in July. Mussolini was forced to step down, and a new administration headed by Marshal Pietro Badoglio took his place. Italy continued to experience military setbacks, and this did little to turn the tide of defeat.

It was obvious that Italy was in danger of failing by the end of the year. The nation was in danger of invasion, its economy was in ruins, and its citizens were growing more and more disenchanted with their leaders. Mussolini had come to represent everything that was wrong with Italy, and his fall appeared inevitable.

CHAPTER XII: THE ALLIES STRIKE BACK

D-DAY

As they prepared for what would be the largest amphibious invasion in history, the Allied forces were extremely busy in the weeks before D-Day. The stakes could not have been higher when the invasion date of June 6th, 1944, was set.

Soldiers from the United States, Great Britain, Canada, and other nations made up the Allied forces. Months prior to the invasion, they meticulously researched the Normandy beaches where they would be landing. The element of surprise, the weather, and the troops' capacity to establish a foothold on the beach were just a few of the variables that would determine the invasion's success.

The Allies ramped up their preparations as the invasion date drew near. The soldiers underwent specialised instruction in amphibious warfare and received practice using landing craft and beach assault strategies.

They learned how to quickly establish a beachhead and, once they had established their position, how to advance inland.

In order to gain air superiority over the Normandy beaches, the air forces participated in the preparations as well. Fighters were tasked with intercepting any German aircraft that attempted to interfere with the invasion, while bombers were sent to destroy German defences and cut off their supply lines.

The Allies started to assemble a massive number of supplies and equipment on the ground. This included everything from artillery and tanks to food and medical supplies. The logistics of the operation required a massive amount of planning, and the Allies had to make sure they had the resources necessary to support their troops after they had landed.

The Allies not only made military preparations but also launched a massive deception campaign. They pretended to be preparing to invade a different region of Europe by building a fake army and outfitting it with inflatable tanks and other tools.

This was done to throw the Germans off guard and keep them guessing as to where the actual invasion would occur.

Tensions were high as the invasion approached. There was a growing sense of unease among the troops as a result of the unpredictable weather conditions. Everything had to go according to plan for the invasion to succeed, and any unforeseen circumstances could potentially ruin the whole thing.

The Allies continued with their preparations despite the difficulties. They understood that the success of the invasion was crucial to the future of Europe and that they had to exert every effort to make that happen.

The invasion's scope was astounding. Along with thousands of ships and aeroplanes, there were more than 150,000 soldiers involved. The Allies had planned the invasion for months, researching the Normandy beaches where they would be landing, and preparing for every conceivable contingency.

The German defence was ferocious and unrelenting as the invasion got underway. The German soldiers were adamant about repelling the invasion at all costs, and the beaches of Normandy were heavily fortified.

When the soldiers arrived on the beaches, they encountered a scene of unspeakable horror. The soldiers battled for their lives against ferocious resistance from the German defenders as the sound of gunfire and explosions filled the air.

Chaos and devastation could be seen all over the beach. The bodies of fallen soldiers were scattered across the sand, and the sea was stained red with blood. As the soldiers continued to fight, determined to overcome the German resistance and establish a foothold on the beach, the air was thick with the smell of burning flesh and gunpowder.

The Allied soldiers persevered in their fight with incredible bravery and tenacity in the face of the appalling circumstances. They understood that the outcome of the invasion would depend on their ability to get past German defences and establish a beachhead on the coast. They also understood that the fate of Europe was on the line.

The battle's momentum started to shift in the Allies' favour as the day went on. They managed to establish a foothold on the beach and started to advance inland, pushing past the German defences.

The soldiers who fought on the beaches of Normandy would never forget the horrors they had witnessed that day. No human being should ever have to witness the scene of bloodshed and devastation.

But despite the atrocities of that day, the Allied troops won. The pendulum had swung back in the allies' favour with Churchill and Eisenhower eager to press further inland after the invasion of Normandy, which was the first allied pushback into mainland Europe and occupied German territory.

THE WESTERN FRONT

The Allied forces continued their advance through Western Europe after the successful D-Day landings on June 6, 1944. After securing the Normandy beaches, the Allies started to advance inland, battling the German forces that were frantically attempting to hold onto their territory.

The Germans mounted a mighty defence during the initial push, making it challenging. The French countryside's hedgerows and winding roads made it challenging for the Allies to advance, and the German forces took full advantage of this, causing the Allies to sustain significant losses.

The Allied forces made progress in spite of these setbacks. While the British and Canadian forces under General Bernard Montgomery advanced eastward from the Gold, Juno, and Sword beaches, the American forces under General Omar Bradley advanced inland from the Omaha and Utah beaches.

The German defences were finally breached by the Allied forces at the town of Saint-Lô on July 25, 1944, leaving a hole. With this success, the Allies were able to seriously start their advance through France.

The German forces put up a fierce fight against the Allies as they advanced. The Germans were determined to keep their control of their territory at all costs, and they had constructed a number of defensive lines, including the infamous Siegfried Line.

To breach these defences, the Allies combined air power, artillery, and infantry. They also utilised their advantage in tanks, with the American Sherman tank proving to be especially effective against the German Panther and Tiger tanks.

A number of towns and cities that had been occupied by the Germans for many years were freed as the Allies advanced. The French people enthusiastically welcomed the Allied forces, and the Allied soldiers were hailed as heroes.

On August 19, 1944, the French Resistance revolted against the German forces occupying the city, marking the beginning of Paris' liberation. The Resistance was well-equipped and well-organised because they had been months in the making. They started attacking German troops and facilities all over the city, and soon gunfire could be heard resonating through the streets.

The sudden uprising caught the German forces off guard, and they initially tried to use force to repress the Resistance. They opened fire on civilian crowds, and there were reports of the executions of alleged Resistance fighters in cold blood.

The Resistance remained strong in the face of these brutal measures. They fought with a steely determination that caught the Germans off guard because they were determined to free their city from German occupation.

The Allied forces outside of Paris prepared to launch a full-scale assault as the fighting in the city intensified.

Under General Jacques Leclerc's direction, the 4th Infantry Division of the United States and the 2nd Armoured Division of France were assigned to lead the assault.

The attack on the city by the Allies started on August 24. The Allied attack was so massive that despite the German forces' valiant efforts, they were ultimately defeated. As they moved steadily through the city, the Americans and French liberated neighbourhood after neighbourhood.

The American and French forces arrived in the city's centre early on August 25. As they passed through the streets, they were greeted by jubilant crowds of civilians who threw flowers and gave the soldiers hugs.

Although the German forces had largely left the city, Paris still had some isolated areas of resistance. The battle raged on for several more days, with the remaining German soldiers putting up a valiant fight against the Allied forces.

The last German soldiers in Paris finally gave up on August 29. The city had been entirely freed, and the Allied forces had won a crucial battle.

The war's pivotal event was the liberation of Paris. It demonstrated both the strength of the Allies' forces and the tenacity of the French people. It also provided the French people, who had endured years of German occupation, with a much-needed morale boost.

The Allied forces in Europe were making significant progress by the fall of 1944. The Supreme Commander of the Allied Forces, General Dwight D. Eisenhower, had devised a daring strategy to end the war quickly. Operation Market Garden was an ambitious attempt to seize important Dutch bridges and create a route into Germany.

Thousands of paratroopers were dropped behind enemy lines during the operation, which involved the largest airborne drop in history, to secure the bridges. So that the Allied forces could advance into Germany, the ground forces would move swiftly to join up with the paratroopers and secure the bridges.

Thousands of paratroopers jumped into the Netherlands to start the operation on September 17, 1944. The initial landings were successful, and the paratroopers were able to take control of important bridges and repel German counterattacks.

However, the ground forces encountered difficult opposition. The British XXX Corps encountered fierce German resistance while attempting to advance up the main road towards the city of Arnhem and sustained significant losses.

The operation went on despite this setback. The Allied forces were able to advance towards Arnhem thanks to the success of the American 82nd and 101st Airborne Divisions in securing the bridges at Nijmegen and Eindhoven.

The Allied troops could not be reinforced or resupplied on the ground because the German forces were able to cut off their supply lines. After being dropped at Arnhem, the British 1st Airborne Division was eventually encircled and made to submit.

The Allies were ultimately unsuccessful in securing the last bridge at Arnhem, making the operation a failure. With over 17,000 Allied soldiers killed, wounded, or captured, there were significant losses.

A major setback for the Allied forces was Operation Market Garden's failure. The German forces had more time to reassemble and reorganise as a result of the delay in the allied advance into Germany.

Despite the operation's failure, it showed the bravery and valour of the Allied forces. Despite the extreme danger and unpredictability they faced when they descended behind enemy lines, the paratroopers remained devoted to their mission. Despite suffering significant losses, the ground forces kept moving forward and fought for every inch of territory.

GERMANY'S FINAL OFFENSIVE

The Allied forces in Europe were on the attack in the winter of 1944. They were moving towards Germany after liberating Paris. The German army, however, was far from being vanquished.

In what would come to be known as the Battle of the Bulge, they launched a significant counterattack in Belgium's Ardennes.

The Allies were unprepared for the German offensive. Poor weather made it challenging for Allied air support to conduct operations. Additionally, the Germans had gathered a sizable number of soldiers and tanks, which they used to breach the Allied defences.

Over a month of fighting ensued, with significant casualties on both sides. Despite being forced back, the Allied forces were eventually able to regroup and launch their own counterattack.

The conflict was important for a variety of reasons. It was the German army's final significant offensive of the war and a last-ditch effort to change the course of the conflict in their favour. Due to the bad weather, the Allies were unable to provide the necessary support, which further highlighted the significance of air power in modern warfare.

The war's turning point was another important aspect of the Battle of the Bulge. The German army's resources were depleted as a result of being pushed back on all sides. The German army was further depleted by the battle's staggering losses, and they were never able to mount another significant offensive.

The Allied forces showed incredible resiliency and resolve despite the setbacks. After reorganising, they were able to launch a counterattack that drove the Germans back. The conflict served as a testament to the bravery and valour displayed by the soldiers on both sides.

The Bulge was important because it illustrated the value of intelligence in contemporary warfare. The Allies were able to intercept and decode German communications because they had broken the German code. As a result, they were able to predict the German movements and make strategic plans that gave them a significant tactical advantage.

The Battle of the Bulge ultimately cost both sides a lot of money. Massive losses were sustained by the German army, and they were never able to recover.

Even though the Allied forces were thin, they were able to regroup and carry on with their advance towards Germany.

After the Battle of the Bulge, Allied forces started moving in the direction of the Rhine, a crucial physical barrier in Germany. It was challenging for the Allies to cross because the Germans had fortified the area knowing this. The Allies, however, were adamant about continuing their march towards Berlin after crossing the Rhine.

Operation Varsity, a significant airborne operation that involved dropping over 16,000 paratroopers and gliders behind enemy lines, was launched by the Allies in March 1945. The operation's goal was to establish a bridgehead across the Rhine so that the Allied forces could cross and advance further towards Germany's industrial core.

The Allies were successful in securing the bridgehead despite a strong German resistance, and by the end of March they had crossed the Rhine and were moving towards Berlin. The Allies were committed to putting an end to the war, while the Germans were currently engaged in a desperate defensive struggle.

As the Allies moved closer to Berlin, the German army fiercely resisted them. Both sides suffered numerous casualties as a result of the intense fighting. The Allies, however, persisted in their advance, and by April 1945, they had encircled Berlin and were drawing near the city.

THE EASTERN FRONT

The war on the Eastern Front had turned in favour of the Soviet Union by the beginning of 1944. They had been successful in forcing the German army back into Germany while capturing city after city in the process. The Germans, however, weren't going down without a fight. They continued to launch a counteroffensive against the Soviet Union and remained a formidable foe.

The Battle of Narva, which took place in the Estonian city of Narva in February and March of 1944, was one of the most important events on the Eastern Front during this time. When the German army launched a massive offensive against the Soviet Union, the conflict started. In order to retake control of the Baltic region, they aimed to push the Soviet Union back.

The German army was well-prepared for the offensive and had a sizable technological and firepower advantage.

The Soviet Union, however, was not going down without a fight. They were committed to resisting the German offensive and holding their ground. In terms of the quantity of soldiers present on the ground, the Soviet Union held a commanding advantage and was well-equipped for the conflict.

Both sides suffered numerous casualties as a result of the brutal and intense fighting. The German army launched attack after attack against the Soviet Union as the conflict continued for weeks. The Soviet Union, on the other hand, was able to maintain their position and launched a number of counter offensives against the German army.

The Soviet Union was able to win the conflict despite the fierce fighting. They were successful in driving the German army back while capturing sizable amounts of land. The German army was compelled to flee and sustained heavy casualties in terms of personnel and supplies.

The Battle of Narva was an important turning point in the Eastern Front war. It demonstrated the Soviet Union's strength as an adversary and the invulnerability of the German army. As the Soviet Union was able to use their superior tactics and preparation to gain the upper hand in the battle, the battle also demonstrated the significance of strategic planning and preparation in warfare.

The Soviet Union achieved a significant victory at the Battle of Narva, which opened the door for them to continue their advance on Germany. The German army suffered a significant setback as well, proving that they were unable to hold their own against the Soviet Union.

The German army put up a valiant fight against the Soviet Union as they advanced towards Germany. The Germans gave it their all in an effort to halt the Red Army's advance. They could not, however, compete with the superior military power of the Soviet Union.

Operation Bagration was the Soviet Union's biggest offensive yet against the Nazis in July and August of 1944.

On June 22, 1944, the operation got underway with the intention of driving the German army from the Soviet Union and liberating Eastern Europe. Pyotr Bagration, a Napoleonic War hero who died in battle in 1812, inspired the operation's name.

The operation was started by the Soviet Union with a ground invasion and a heavy artillery barrage. The Soviet Union managed to surprise the German army by launching the attack from a number of different angles. The German army was quickly outnumbered, and they lost a sizable number of personnel and weapons.

During the operation, the Soviet Union was able to gain important ground and seize a sizable portion of German-held territory. They succeeded in driving the German army from Belarus and Ukraine and advanced on Poland. Both sides suffered significant losses as a result of the operation.

Operation Bagration was a success for a variety of reasons. The Soviet Union had the advantage in numbers, and they were able to make excellent use of their tanks and artillery.

Additionally, they were able to sabotage German communications and supply routes by using their air force. The Soviet Union also had better coordination and planning skills, which enabled them to launch a coordinated attack from a number of different angles.

The offensive, which was the largest military operation of the conflict, dealt the German army a fatal blow. The Soviet Union continued to advance towards Berlin as the Germans were forced to retreat.

The German's resistance to the Soviet Union's advance on Germany became more and more ferocious. The Germans gave it their all in an effort to halt the Red Army's advance. But it was becoming obvious that the Soviet Union would prevail on the Eastern Front.

Stalin launched his final significant offensive against Germany in 1945 before they reached the capital. The Vistula-Oder Offensive was launched with the intention of driving the German army from Poland and ultimately putting an end to the European War.

On January 12, 1945, a significant artillery barrage against German positions along the Vistula River signalled the start of the offensive. The Soviet Union moved swiftly past the German defences and in the direction of the Oder River.

The Soviet Union's superior numbers and firepower caught the German army off guard and quickly overpowered them. Warsaw and Poznan were among the significant cities the Soviet Union was able to seize, and they continued their advance on Berlin.

HITLER'S FAILED WAR

Adolf Hitler's mental state grew more erratic and unstable as the Second World War came to an end. Hitler's mental health suffered greatly during the Nazi regime's string of crises and setbacks in the years 1944–1955.

A daring plot to kill Adolf Hitler and overthrow the Nazi government was launched in July 1944 by a group of German officers under the command of Colonel Claus von Stauffenberg.

One of the most dramatic incidents of the Second World War, the Operation Valkyrie plot had a significant influence on Hitler and the course of the conflict.

A number of reasons, including the perception among some German officers that the war was lost, and that Hitler's rule was bringing the nation to ruin, served as the inspiration for the plot. Conservative nationalists who opposed Hitler's more extreme policies, such as his anti-Semitic laws and his plans for the conquest of Europe, made up a large portion of the conspirators.

The strategy was straightforward: Stauffenberg would detonate a bomb at Hitler's East Prussian headquarters, where Hitler was slated to hold a meeting. Hitler would be killed, and the government would fall into disarray when the bomb was remotely detonated. The conspirators believed this would open the door for a coup and the installation of a new administration that would file a request for peace with the Allies.

But when the bomb only partially detonated and failed to kill Hitler, the assassination attempt was a failure.

Hitler survived despite being hurt and was able to reclaim control of the German government. The conspirators and a large number of their supporters were swiftly apprehended and put to death.

Operation Valkyrie had a significant effect on Hitler and the Nazi government. The assassination attempt severely rattled Hitler, shattering his sense of invincibility and making him even more paranoid about potential challenges to his authority. He grew more withdrawn and wary of his subordinates, depending more and more on his inner circle of devoted followers.

Hitler's mental state rapidly deteriorated as the allies were about to enter Berlin. He spent most of his time in his Berlin bunker, which led to his increasing isolation and delusion. To keep himself going, he became more and more dependent on drugs and stimulants, such as cocaine and amphetamines. His mental health was severely affected by this, leaving him with hallucinations, paranoia, and insomnia.

Hitler clung to the idea that victory was still attainable throughout the war's final days.

Even as their cause grew increasingly hopeless, he refused to consider any type of surrender and instead ordered his troops to continue fighting. He became more unpredictable and irrational, giving contradictory instructions and uttering evermore bizarre statements.

In his final days, Hitler became increasingly detached from reality. He refused to believe that the war was lost and became obsessed with conspiracy theories about the Allied powers and the Jews. He reportedly suffered from bouts of uncontrollable rage and would lash out at those around him for the slightest perceived slights.

CHAPTER XIII: THE ITALIAN FALLOUT

Italy was left without a clear leader after Mussolini's departure, and the political environment was unstable. Adolf Hitler, the head of Nazi Germany, was closely monitoring what was happening in Italy and waiting for the appropriate time to act.

Mussolini was removed from office as prime minister by Italian King Victor Emmanuel III on July 25, 1943. Later, he was arrested and held captive in Northern Italy. The action was taken following months of Italy's political and military defeats, which included the loss of North Africa to the Allies. Many Italians blamed Mussolini for the nation's issues as he lost favour with the populace. Pietro Badoglio, who took his position, was viewed as a more moderate leader who would be able to broker a deal with the Allies.

But the new administration rapidly encountered problems and fell short of its objectives.

The lack of legitimacy of the new government was one of its key issues. By negotiating the surrender to the Allies, Badoglio gained the ire of many Italians as a traitor who had worked with the enemy. The fact that Badoglio had been a significant figure in Mussolini's fascist government, which had dominated Italy for more than 20 years, added to this impression. As a result, the new government's authority was compromised, and it was unable to garner the support of the Italian people.

The military situation was still another important concern. Italy's armed forces were in disarray as a result of a string of disastrous losses, notably the loss of North Africa. Italy continued to experience defeats on the battlefield as the new government failed to change the course of the war.

The management of the economy presented substantial difficulties for the new government as well. Italy depended largely on imports, and the Allied blockade made it challenging to obtain the essential supplies. Italians suffered from shortages and inflation since the new government was unable to resolve these issues.

The oyster Mussolini served up did not delight Hitler. He believed that without the Italian leader, Italy may submit to the Allies since he considered the latter as a crucial ally in his goals for hegemony over Europe. Martin Bormann, Hitler's chief advisor, was promptly dispatched to Italy to examine the situation and attempt to persuade Mussolini to exercise his authority once more.

On August 1, 1943, barely one week after Mussolini was ousted, Bormann landed in Italy. He met with Mussolini, who was being detained by the Italian government, and urged him to assume command. After some hesitation, Mussolini decided to join with Bormann to create a new government.

THE ALLIED INVASION OF ITALY

During World War II, the Allied invasion of Italy marked a turning point in the conflict. The invasion, which was a joint effort of the United States and Great Britain, had the objectives of creating a new front in Europe, diverting German forces from other battlefronts, and finally putting an end to the European conflict.

In Italy's Calabria on September 3, 1943, the Allies made landfall. The landing was a part of Operation Avalanche, a bigger operation that saw more than 80,000 Allied soldiers arrive on the Italian mainland as part of a joint operation between the United States and Great Britain.

The Allied invasion of Italy marked a turning point in the conflict. The invasion, which was a joint effort of the United States and Great Britain, had the objectives of creating a new front in Europe, diverting German forces from other battlefronts, and finally putting an end to the European conflict.

Due to their inadequate equipment and low morale from years of combat, the Italian soldiers initially offered only little resistance to the landing. The Allies moved swiftly to seize the area before moving inland.

The German forces, who had received reinforcements from other regions of Europe, put up more fight as the Allies advanced further north. It was challenging to drive the Germans out of their positions because they had strengthened them in anticipation of an Allied invasion.

As they advanced up the Italian peninsula, the Allies encountered rugged terrain, ferocious resistance, and challenging weather. German mines and booby traps were set to impede the Allies' approach along the entrenched positions dotting the Italian coastline.

At the Battle of Salerno, when they ran across fierce German opposition, the Allies suffered their first significant defeat. The Allies sustained significant losses during the prolonged combat, which lasted several days. Nevertheless, they were ultimately successful in holding their position and moving northward.

Despite these obstacles, the Allies continued to make progress towards their eventual objective of conquering Naples. The city, which had a significant strategic port, would serve as a basis for subsequent Allied operations in Italy.

Italy switched sides in the war in October 1943 when the new administration under Pietro Badoglio negotiated an armistice with the Allies. But the German forces in Italy resisted capitulation and started a huge counteroffensive against the Italian forces right away.

The Germans and the few remaining Italian forces still supporting Mussolini presented the Allies with a two-front conflict.

The Allies fought their way north through a number of challenging encounters as they resumed the fight for Italy over the winter of 1943–1944. Field Marshal Albert Kesselring's German forces were challenging to drive out because they had dug in and strengthened their positions.

In the spring of 1944, as the Allies attempted to breach the German defences at the Gustav Line, they encountered some of the most difficult fighting of the war. The Germans were adamant about keeping control of the line, which consisted of several strongly fortified positions. Despite suffering significant losses during the conflict, the Allies were eventually able to make progress.

The Allies had reached Rome by the summer of 1944, but the Germans were still putting up a valiant fight. As they advanced further north, the Allies captured town after town. The Germans were determined to make every inch of ground costly to the Allies, meaning advancement was slow.

THE DEATH OF MUSSOLINI

After speaking with Bormann, a group of German paratroopers under the command of Otto Skorzeny launched a daring rescue operation to free Mussolini from captivity on September 12, 1943. Mussolini was flown to Germany to meet with Adolf Hitler after the mission was successful.

The goal of Mussolini's visit to Germany was to demonstrate the Axis powers' strength and unity. The German people, who viewed Mussolini as a symbol of the Axis cause, treated him as a hero and gave him a warm welcome.

Mussolini met with Hitler and other senior Nazi officials during his visit. They talked about their strategies for winning the war and how they could keep cooperating to defeat the Allies. In Germany, Mussolini also met with Italian expatriates and urged them to continue fighting for the Axis.

The Axis powers saw Mussolini's trip to Germany as a propaganda victory.

Media coverage of the meeting between Mussolini and Hitler was intense, and the German people were informed of the Axis powers' continued strength and unity in the face of the Allies.

Mussolini's trip to Germany was not without issues, though. Mussolini was aware that, despite his hero status, his influence in the war was waning. He had lost the support of the Italian people, and his government had fallen. Mussolini was also conscious of his growing reliance on German assistance, making him feel inferior as a leader.

Mussolini was to be appointed as the head of the Italian Social Republic, a puppet state set up by the Germans in northern Italy, per Hitler's decision. Germany and other Axis nations formally recognised Mussolini's new regime, but the Allies and the Italian people never did.

Numerous issues plagued Mussolini's new government right away. Due to its isolation and lack of resources and assistance, the Italian Social Republic was unable to wage the war successfully.

Internal conflicts and divisions between Mussolini's supporters and other factions also plagued the nation.

Despite these difficulties, Mussolini remained in charge of the Italian Social Republic, participating actively in the war effort and appearing in front of the public frequently. But as the war wore on, it became obvious that Mussolini's regime was unsustainable, and it started to fall.

Benito Mussolini realised his time was limited in April 1945 as the Allied forces drew closer to taking the whole of Italy and the end of World War II drew near. He was sought after by the Italian resistance and the Allies because his fascist government had fallen.

Mussolini devised a plan to escape capture in an effort to reach Switzerland, where he hoped to find refuge and perhaps even carry on the war against the Allies. He asked Count Galeazzo Ciano, a friend and former foreign minister, who was being detained by the Germans, to assist in organising his escape.

Edda Ciano, a participant in the scheme, set up a plane to transport Mussolini and a group of his supporters to the Swiss border using her connections with the Germans. Captain Heinrich Gerlach, a German officer who had previously served under Mussolini, was in charge of flying the aircraft.

Mussolini and his entourage left Milan in a convoy of cars on April 27, 1945, with the intention of meeting the plane at a small airfield in northern Italy. After navigating checkpoints and roadblocks set up by the Allies throughout the night, they arrived at the airfield in the early morning.

The strategy, however, quickly started to fall apart. The Germans were keeping a close eye on the airfield because they had heard about the attempted escape and were waiting for Mussolini. Captain Gerlach, who had previously been implicated in a plot against Hitler, aroused the suspicion of the Germans, who detained both him and his co-pilot.

Mussolini and his supporters had no way to leave the airfield and were left stranded there.

They were quickly apprehended and taken into custody by Italian partisans who had been informed about their attempted escape.

Mussolini's last-ditch effort to flee to Switzerland ultimately failed. He miscalculated the Germans' resolve to capture him and the organisation of his poorly thought-out plan. As the war came to an end, the Italians had also turned against him, and chaos reigned throughout the nation.

Mussolini was brought to the village of Dongo and imprisoned in a little villa. Along with his mistress, Clara Petacci, he was executed by firing squad on April 28, 1945.

Italy and the rest of the world quickly learned of Mussolini's passing, and many people rejoiced at the end of the war and the fascist regime. Others, however, lamented Mussolini's passing and regarded him as a hero and a representation of Italian pride.

The news of Mussolini's passing was received with mixed feelings in Milan. Numerous people celebrated in the streets, but there were also fascist organisations that were adamant about paying tribute to Mussolini's memory and supporting his legacy.

Mussolini's body was taken control of by a group of fascist supporters, led by Rodolfo Graziani, who then started organising a funeral procession through Milan. They put Mussolini's body in a truck, draped it in the Italian flag, and started the procession, which quickly descended into an unruly and bloody event.

Fascists and anti-fascist protesters clashed as the procession moved through Milan's streets, and the police struggled to keep things under control. When some of Mussolini's supporters started firing guns into the air, creating panic and mayhem in the streets, the situation worsened.

The procession carried on despite the violence and mayhem and eventually arrived at Milan's Piazzale Loreto.

The bodies of Mussolini and his mistress, Clara Petacci, were hung from a petrol station roof by the fascists.

Many Italians were shocked to see Mussolini's body hanging in the open, and it signalled the end of the fascist era. A period of political and social reform that aimed to create a new, democratic Italy was quickly launched by the government in an effort to distance itself from Mussolini and the fascist legacy.

Mussolini's failed attempt to flee to Switzerland brought about the tragic demise of a once-powerful leader. His attempt to flee only added to the mayhem of the war's closing days, and his dream of a fascist Italy had come to an end in failure. Mussolini is now regarded as a cautionary example of the perils of totalitarianism and the results of leading a country down a destructive path.

CHAPTER XIV: THE END OF WAR IN EUROPE

The Second World War in Europe would finally come to an end in the spring of 1945. While the Western Allies fought their way through France, Belgium, and the Netherlands, the Red Army of the Soviet Union had been steadily moving eastward towards Germany.

By April, the Red Army had made it to Berlin's outskirts, Nazi Germany's capital. Over 100,000 German soldiers were stationed in the city to defend it, and they were prepared to fight to the death.

With significant casualties on both sides, the battle for Berlin was one of the bloodiest and most brutal of the entire Second World War. Months prior to the battle, the Germans fortified the city and sent over 100,000 soldiers to guard it. They were up against overwhelming odds, though, as the Red Army had access to significantly more soldiers, tanks, and artillery.

The conflict started in April 1945 when the Red Army launched an all-out assault on the city. To try to get past the German defences, they used infantry, artillery, and tanks. The fighting was ferocious, with both sides engaged in intense street-to-street fighting.

The Germans put up a strong fight, employing all available strategies to halt the Soviet advance. To repel the Soviet troops, they set up mines, booby traps, and barriers throughout the city, along with snipers and machine guns.

The Germans fought valiantly and employed every trick in their arsenal to hold them back, causing the Red Army to suffer significant losses. The Germans were forced to retreat from some areas of the city as a result of the Soviet Union's massive air raids and artillery barrages, which left extensive damage in their wake.

The Germans put up a strong fight, employing all available strategies to halt the Soviet advance. To repel the Soviet troops, they set up mines, booby traps, and barriers throughout the city, along with snipers and machine guns.

The Red Army faced heavy losses, as the Germans fought tenaciously and used every tactic they could to hold them back. The Soviets responded with massive artillery barrages and air raids, which caused widespread destruction and forced the Germans to retreat further and further into the city.

The Red Army persisted in moving forward despite suffering significant losses, making a slow but steady advance towards the city's centre. They engaged the remaining German defenders in a brutal battle as they made their way through the suburbs and into the city centre.

Adolf Hitler and a select group of advisers, including his long-time partner Eva Braun, withdrew to their underground bunker beneath the Reich Chancellery building in the middle of Berlin as the battle raged outside.

Hitler's mental and physical situation had been deteriorating for some time. He was prone to rage and despair outbursts, and he had developed an increasing sense of paranoia and delusion.

Parkinson's disease, which made it difficult for him to control his movements and left him in constant pain.

Hitler withdrew to his personal quarters in the bunker on April 30, 1945, knowing that the Red Army was only a few blocks away. Instead of being captured by the enemy, he made the decision to end his own life. After a quick wedding ceremony, Hitler and Eva Braun moved to his study to write his last will and testament.

A gunshot was heard from the study at around 3:30 p.m. When Heinz Linge, Hitler's valet, walked into the room, he discovered Hitler slumped over his desk with a gunshot wound to the head. He was lying next to Eva Braun, who had also been shot to death. Hitler's body was carried up to the Reich Chancellery building's garden where it was set ablaze in a hastily built funeral pyre.

The official German army's surrender on May 1 marked the end of World War II in Europe. People all over the world were relieved to hear that the war had finally come to an end as the news quickly spread.

The people of Germany were shocked, and many were left to wonder what would happen to their nation. Most Germans were completely unprepared for the news of the surrender as they had been informed that the war was progressing well, and that victory was imminent. In reality, for several weeks prior to the announcement of the surrender, the German government had been in secret talks to end the war.

The news was welcomed with relief and joy in other parts of Europe. People were finally able to exhale in relief and start rebuilding their lives after years of bombing, occupation, and constant fighting.

The news was received with a mixture of relief and happiness in the US and UK. Both nations had suffered greatly as a result of the war, and the public was eager to welcome their soldiers back and kick off the reconstruction process.

But the end of the war was a bittersweet experience for many people. Numerous other lives had also suffered irreparable harm, and millions of lives had been lost. Never again would the world be the same.

People started to adjust to the new reality in the weeks and months that followed. Although the process of rebuilding would be protracted and challenging, people were committed to making progress.

In particular the German people had a difficult task ahead of them. Years of war had decimated the nation, leaving its infrastructure in ruins. However, they began the drawn-out process of reconstruction with the assistance of the Allies.

The end of the war provided a sense of closure for the families of the soldiers who had died fighting. Finally, they could start to grieve and accept the loss of their loved ones.

The conclusion of World War II in Europe and the German peace treaty ultimately marked a turning point in world history. The world had been forever altered by the war, and its effects would last for countless years to come. However, the end of the war provided many with a sense of hope and the prospect of a better future.

THE WAR IN THE PACIFIC

CHAPTER XV: THE ROAD TO WAR

JAPANESE EXPANSION

It was the summer of 1937 when Japan invaded China, sparking a brutal eight-year conflict that would have far-reaching consequences for the region and the world. However, this was only the beginning of the Japanese military's aspirations. They had their sights set on extending their empire into the vast Pacific Ocean, beyond the Chinese mainland.

The idea of the "Greater East Asia Co-Prosperity Sphere," which was at the centre of Japan's strategy, was firmly held. This was an idea of a new order in Asia, where Japan would assume the position of leader of a group of countries and peoples working together on a common mission of political and economic cooperation. The reality is that this was merely a thinly veiled justification for Japan's imperialistic ambitions, as they sought to establish dominance over the area and secure essential resources for their expanding economy.

With China firmly under their control, Japan turned their attention to the Pacific islands. In September 1940, they invaded French Indochina. The region, which included present-day Vietnam, Laos, and Cambodia, was rich in rubber, oil, and tin, and Japan saw it as a key target in their imperial ambitions.

Japan had given the French government an ultimatum in July of that year, requesting that they permit Japanese troops to occupy the northern part of Indochina. The German occupation of France had already made the French defenceless, so they reluctantly complied with the demand.

The Japanese wasted no time in exploiting the predicament. They began sending troops and supplies into the area just a few days after the agreement, and soon built up a significant presence in the major cities of Hanoi and Saigon. In order to prepare for a prolonged occupation, they also started constructing airfields and other infrastructure.

However, the Japanese were not satisfied with merely controlling Indochina.

They established a network of mines and factories to extract rubber and other materials for their own use in order to seize control of the area's valuable resources. The local population was forced to sell their goods at low prices and was denied access to foreign markets as a result of the strict regulations they imposed on trade and commerce.

Concern among the Allies, especially the United States, grew as word of the Japanese invasion spread. The Americans reacted by imposing economic sanctions on Japan, including an embargo on oil and other essential resources, because they saw Japan's actions as a direct threat to their own interests in the region.

The Japanese economy was dealt a serious blow by this. Japan's military and expanding industrial base depended heavily on imported oil, and the loss of this supply posed a serious threat to the nation's ability to wage war.

The embargo was met with outrage from the Japanese government, branding it an act of aggression and vowed to retaliate.

Following this, tensions between the two countries grew even more tense as Japan took more aggressive measures to reaffirm its power in the Pacific.

The embargo was a contentious decision, and some opponents contended that it would only serve to incite Japan and possibly spark a full-scale conflict. But even if it meant running the risk of a military conflict, President Franklin D. Roosevelt and his advisors were convinced that it was necessary to take a strong stance against Japan's aggression.

Japan grew increasingly irritated with the embargo as the months went by. The government started looking into other oil and material sources, including the Soviet Union, but these endeavours largely failed. Japan was forced to continue its aggressive expansion in the hope that a show of force would persuade the US to lift the embargo.

Japan, Germany, and Italy formalised their alliance by signing the Tripartite Agreement in September 1940.

The United States, which had been paying close attention to Japan's aggressive expansionism in the Pacific, found this agreement to be deeply concerning.

The Tripartite Agreement, which could result in a coordinated military offensive against the United States and its allies, was seen by the American government as a direct threat to its interests in national security. The American government responded by taking a number of steps to lessen the perceived threat.

By freezing Japanese assets in the US, the US government imposed new sanctions on Japan, which greatly incensed the Japanese government. These actions were taken with the intention of destroying Japan's economy and compelling it to give up its expansionist aspirations. By denying Japan access to necessary resources, the American government hoped to deter Japan from pursuing its territorial ambitions and possibly avert a military conflict.

Japan now was faced with an ultimatum - continue their territorial expansion in South Asia and be crippled by US economic sanctions, or face the beast of the American military head on. Admiral Yamamoto opted for the latter and turned his sights towards the Hawaiian naval base known as Pearl Harbour.

PEARL HARBOUR

By 1941, many Americans saw Japan as a belligerent aggressor that needed to be contained, while many Japanese viewed the United States as an imperialist power that was intent on thwarting their country's legitimate aspirations.

Japan started making preparations for its attack on Pearl Harbor against this backdrop of unease and mistrust. Admiral Isoroku Yamamoto, a brilliant strategist, came up with the plan after realising that Japan's only chance of defeating the US was to deliver a decisive blow that would devastate the US Pacific Fleet and force the US to demand peace.

Yamamoto created a daring plan to launch a surprise attack on the American naval base in Pearl Harbor, Hawaii, in order to achieve this goal. In order to destroy as much of the American fleet as possible, the plan called for a massive aerial assault on the harbour using bombers and torpedo planes.

Yamamoto was aware of the plan's inherent danger, but he thought it would be worthwhile given the potential rewards. If the attack is successful, Japan would have a big advantage in the Pacific theatre of the war, which might force the United States to leave the area and give Japan the chance to consolidate its territorial gains.

Only a small group of senior Japanese officials were made aware of the plan for the attack on Pearl Harbor, which was planned in extreme secrecy. Because Yamamoto was concerned that leaks might jeopardise the operation, even many Japanese military leaders were kept in the dark.

Japan was given an ultimatum by the United States in November 1941, asking it to leave China and other occupied territories in the Pacific.

The ultimatum was viewed as a significant escalation in the already present tensions between the two nations, and it created the possibility of a conflict with far-reaching repercussions.

The ultimatum was delivered to the Japanese government by American Ambassador Joseph Grew, who warned that the United States would take strong measures to protect its interests in the Pacific if Japan did not comply with its demands. The ultimatum was couched in diplomatic language, but the underlying message was clear: the United States was prepared to take a tough stance against Japan.

Japan's response to the ultimatum was defiant. The country's leaders viewed the American demands as an affront to their national honour and a threat to their territorial ambitions. Yamamoto was now assured of carrying out the planned attacks.

On December 7, 1941, the Imperial Japanese Navy launched a surprise attack on the United States Pacific Fleet stationed at Pearl Harbor, Hawaii.

The attack dealt the United States a devastating blow and signalled its entry into World War II.

Early in the morning, just before 8:00 am, the first wave of Japanese planes launched their assault. The American defenders were caught off guard when the Japanese planes descended quickly and low. They bombarded the harbour's ships with bombs and torpedoes, severely damaging and destroying them.

The battleship USS Arizona was hit by several bombs before exploding and sinking all within a matter of minutes, killing over 1,000 crew members. Hundreds of sailors were ensnared inside the USS Oklahoma, which was also struck and capsized. The attack also severely damaged the USS California, Nevada, West Virginia, and Utah.

In addition, the Japanese launched attacks on Hickam Field and Wheeler Field, resulting in the ground-based destruction of numerous American aircraft. They also attacked fuel depots and barracks, which resulted in additional destruction and casualties.

Over 2,400 Americans had died and over 1,100 had been injured by the time the attack, which lasted more than two hours, came to an end. The American fleet suffered significant losses, including the destruction or damage of eight battleships, ten other ships, and nearly 200 aircraft.

An important turning point in the war, the attack on Pearl Harbor inspired the American people to join the war effort against Japan and its Axis allies. The following day, President Franklin D. Roosevelt declared war on Japan, referring to December 7, 1941, as "a date which will live in infamy."

The Japanese were successful in their surprise attack on Pearl Harbor, but they fell short in a number of crucial areas. These mistakes would ultimately lead to Japan losing the war.

First of all, because they were not at Pearl Harbor during the attack, the Japanese were unable to destroy the aircraft carriers of the Pacific Fleet. The carriers were a key American asset and were essential to winning the Pacific War.

The Japanese failed to eliminate them, leaving a sizable portion of the American fleet intact and ready to launch reprisal attacks.

Second, the fuel tanks and repair facilities at Pearl Harbor were not harmed or destroyed by the Japanese. The American fleet depended on these facilities to function, and their destruction could have seriously hampered America's ability to fight in the Pacific. However, the Japanese attackers failed to target them, leaving them mostly untouched.

Thirdly, the Japanese grossly underestimated the tenacity of the American people and the military. Although the attack on Pearl Harbor dealt a serious blow to the American fleet, it also strengthened the resolve of the American people to fight back. The day after the attack, the United States declared war on Japan, leading to Japan being at war not only with the United States but also with all of the other Allied powers.

CHAPTER XVI: SIX MONTHS TO WIN

It was a crisp December morning in 1941 when Admiral Isoroku Yamamoto, the commander-in-chief of the Japanese Combined Fleet, received the news that the surprise attack on Pearl Harbor had been a resounding success. The attack had dealt a devastating blow to the United States Navy, destroying or crippling eight battleships, three cruisers, and four destroyers, along with other ships and aircraft.

But Yamamoto was not one to rest on his laurels. He knew that the attack on Pearl Harbor was just the beginning of what would be a long and difficult war with the United States. As he sat in his office, contemplating the events of the day, he made a prediction that would go down in history.

"We have six months to win this war," he said to his staff. "After that, I can give no guarantees."

Yamamoto's prediction was not based on any secret intelligence or inside knowledge of American military capabilities. It was simply a sober assessment of Japan's resources and the challenges they faced in the war. He knew that Japan's navy and air force had dealt a serious blow to the United States, but he also knew that the Americans would not be defeated easily.

THE PHILIPPINES CAMPAIGN

In December 1941, the Japanese launched their assault on the Philippines just hours after the attack on Pearl Harbor. With the American military caught off guard and unprepared, the Japanese quickly gained a foothold in the Philippines, capturing Manila, the capital city, within a few weeks.

General Douglas MacArthur, a legendary figure in American military history, oversaw the American and Filipino forces in the Philippines. Although MacArthur had sworn to protect the Philippines to the death, the situation was dire. His forces were quickly driven back to the Bataan Peninsula, a sliver of land on the western side of the main island of Luzon, because they were outnumbered and outgunned.

The American and Filipino forces on Bataan managed to repel the Japanese for months despite being plagued by illness, malnutrition, and relentless attacks. Both sides suffered significant losses in the brutal and fierce fighting. While the American and Filipino troops were finding it difficult to hold their positions, they remained in the fight in the hopes that reinforcements from the United States would soon arrive.

However, those reinforcements never materialised. The United States was engaged in combat on several fronts, and they lacked the funds to commit a sizable force to the Philippines. Meanwhile, the Japanese were relentless in their attacks, determined to crush the American and Filipino forces on Bataan.

By April 1942, the situation on Bataan was dire. The American and Filipino forces were running low on food, ammunition, and medical supplies. Disease was rampant, with thousands of troops falling ill with malaria and dysentery. Yet they continued to fight on, determined to hold out as long as possible.

General Edward King, in charge of the American and Filipino forces on Bataan, made the difficult choice to surrender on April 9th, 1942. He was aware that further resistance would only cause needless casualties and that his troops were on the verge of disintegrating. The Japanese captured over 76,000 soldiers, including 12,000 Americans and 64,000 Filipinos, and held them as prisoners of war.

The Japanese achieved a significant victory with the surrender of Bataan, which dealt a devastating blow to American morale. Additionally, it signalled the start of the Bataan Death March, one of the war's bloodiest episodes.

From Bataan to a prison camp in northern Luzon, the prisoners were made to march more than 60 miles, suffering from extreme heat, dehydration, and brutal physical abuse.

The prisoners were informed that they would be driven to their destination by truck before the march began at the Mariveles airfield.

The Japanese were compelled to march on foot because they lacked sufficient transportation. The prisoners were made to carry their own tools and personal belongings while receiving no food, water, or medical care.

The conditions on the march were terrible. The sun was scorching, and many of the prisoners had already been weakened by months of malnutrition and disease. The Japanese guards were brutal, beating and killing anyone who fell behind or tried to rest. Many of the prisoners were shot, bayoneted, or beheaded without any warning or explanation.

Additionally, the prisoners experienced a range of physical and mental abuse. Others were made to march in circles or kneel for long periods of time, while some were made to crawl on their hands and knees. Additionally, the Japanese guards engaged in cruel games with the prisoners, such as making them compete for food or water.

Over 10,000 of the inmates had already passed away by the time they arrived at their destination from exhaustion, starvation, or murder.

The survivors were transferred to prison camps, where they endured additional mistreatment and privation. Many were forced to work as slave labourers in mines, factories, or construction sites, frequently in the most dreadful and cruelling conditions.

The Bataan Death March was a war crime of unprecedented brutality. It was a deliberate attempt by the Japanese military to break the spirit and will of the American and Filipino prisoners of war, and it was carried out with ruthless efficiency. The prisoners who made it through the march and subsequent captivity were physically and psychologically scarred for life, and many of them never fully recovered from the ordeal they went through.

The Japanese continued their occupation of the Philippines despite the horrors of the Bataan Death March. They persisted in their campaign of conquest, taking control of additional significant cities and islands spread across the archipelago.

The Fall of Corregidor signalled the end of the Japanese Philippines campaign.

The Japanese forces captured nearly 12,000 American and Filipino soldiers in this bloody and arduous battle that lasted for more than a month.

The Japanese launched a massive attack on Corregidor, a fortified island that served as the last line of defence for the Allies in the Philippines, on April 29, 1942, sparking the start of the conflict. The island was well guarded by more than 13,000 soldiers and numerous artillery batteries, but the Japanese were adamant about capturing it.

The island was subjected to a daily barrage of thousands of artillery shells from the Japanese. The defenders had no choice but to fortify themselves in their bunkers and trenches while enduring relentless shelling and airstrikes. The constant barrage of firepower gradually wore down the Allied forces in spite of their bravery and tenacity.

The Japanese gradually drove the defenders back towards the seaside cliffs as the battle dragged on and they gained ground.

Although their supplies and ammunition were running low and their morale was dwindling, the Allied troops fought bravely, launching counterattacks and repelling Japanese assaults.

Using tanks and flamethrowers to breach the Allied defences, the Japanese launched a massive assault on the eastern part of the island on May 5. The Japanese onslaught was so overwhelming that despite the strong resistance of the defenders, they were ultimately defeated. The eastern sector of the island fell within hours, forcing the defenders to flee to the western part of the island.

The Japanese continued their advance over the following few days, gradually driving the Allied forces back towards the cliffs. The Malinta Tunnel served as the defenders' last bastion before being forced to leave their positions. The tunnel, a vast network of subterranean chambers and corridors, served as the Allied command centre throughout the conflict.

On May 6, the Japanese launched their last attack on the tunnel, using grenades and flamethrowers to push the defenders from their positions.

The Allied soldiers fiercely resisted, but it was in vain. The battle was over after a few hours when the Japanese took control of the tunnel.

The Allied cause in the Philippines suffered a fatal blow with the fall of Corregidor. It signalled the end of the American and Filipino resistance and the start of the Japanese forces' brutal and protracted occupation. Many of the prisoners of war died from disease, starvation, and abuse as a result of the appalling conditions they were kept in.

THE EAST INDIA CAMPAIGN

The Imperial Japanese Army engaged in a number of military operations against the British and Allied forces in Southeast Asia during the Second World War known as the Japanese East India Campaign. The Dutch East Indies, British Malaya, and Burma were all oil-rich nations when the campaign was launched in December 1941.

Within a few weeks, Japanese forces had swept through Southeast Asia, taking Singapore, the Philippines, and the majority of the Dutch East Indies.

In the early stages of the campaign, the British and Allied forces suffered a string of crushing defeats because they were unprepared and caught off guard when confronted by the superior Japanese army.

The Battle of Malaya, which began on December 8th, 1941, was the first significant conflict of the campaign. The British and Commonwealth forces were stationed on the north-eastern coast of the Malay Peninsula, where the invasion began with a massive amphibious assault. With the help of their powerful naval and air forces, the Japanese successfully attacked the British defences with airstrikes and artillery barrages. The British had been expecting an attack, but they were caught off guard by the ferocity of the Japanese assault.

The Japanese took command of the air and the sea very quickly, and they made use of this to their advantage by beginning a series of amphibious landings along the coast. The British forces were forced to retreat southward towards Singapore as they were greatly outnumbered and outgunned.

The Japanese advanced quickly, and within a week, they had taken control of the important towns of Kota Bharu and Kuantan and were making their way towards Kuala Lumpur.

Japanese strategies that combined speed, mobility, and surprise allowed them to get past British defences. While their infantry attacked from the flanks and rear, the Japanese used tanks, armoured cars, and artillery to breach the British defences. The Japanese assault quickly overpowered the British troops, who were ill-equipped and poorly trained.

The Japanese had already established a clear advantage as the British and Commonwealth forces attempted to reorganise and launch a counterattack. The challenging terrain and inclement weather hindered the British troops, who were also worn out and demoralised.

The British forces offered little resistance to the Japanese as they advanced towards Singapore. The Japanese took control of the main road and rail link to Singapore after capturing the important town of Ipoh.

With their backs to the sea, the British were now stranded on the southernmost point of the Malay Peninsula.

Massive artillery bombardment and a series of amphibious landings on Singapore's northern coast were used by the Japanese to launch their assault. The Japanese were able to launch airstrikes and torpedo attacks on the British defences with great efficiency thanks to their superior air and naval power.

The British forces put up a valiant fight, but the Japanese assault quickly outnumbered them. To breach the British defences, the Japanese used a combination of tanks, artillery, and infantry. Due to their inadequate training and equipment, the British forces were unable to withstand the Japanese attack's ferocity.

The Japanese made rapid progress and captured several key positions on the island, including the Alexandra Hospital, which was the largest hospital in Singapore. The Japanese also cut off the water supply to the city, which led to widespread panic and chaos.

The British forces tried to counterattack, but their efforts were hampered by the difficult terrain and harsh weather conditions. The Japanese continued their advance, and within a matter of days, they had reached the outskirts of the city.

The British army made their last stand in the city centre after retreating back into it. The British defences were breached by the Japanese after they launched a powerful attack on the city that combined airstrikes, tank assaults, and infantry assaults.

Although they fought valiantly, the British forces were utterly outgunned and outnumbered. Japanese soldiers broke into the city's core and started fighting with British soldiers on the streets. Both sides suffered significant losses in the brutal and intense fighting.

The British forces were running low on supplies and ammunition, and their morale was low. The Japanese, on the other hand, were well-supplied and well-trained, and they continued to advance relentlessly.

On February 15th, 1942, Lieutenant General Arthur Percival was forced to surrender, marking the largest surrender of British forces in history. The fall of Singapore was a devastating blow to the British and Commonwealth forces, and it marked the beginning of the end of the British Empire.

The Japanese launched the Burma Campaign in 1942, spurred on by their apparent invincibility in the Pacific. This was one of the most brutal and gruelling campaigns of World War II. It was fought between the Allied forces, led by the British, and the Japanese Imperial Army in the jungles and mountains of Burma.

The campaign began in 1942 when the Japanese invaded Burma and quickly captured Rangoon, the capital. The British forces, led by General Archibald Wavell, were taken by surprise, and they were forced to retreat northward towards the Indian border.

The Japanese forces were ruthless and determined, employing a combination of superior tactics, technology, and training to defeat the British forces.

The jungle terrain and harsh weather conditions made the fighting even more difficult, with both sides suffering from disease, exhaustion, and starvation.

The British forces attempted to reorganise and launch a counteroffensive, but they encountered supply, reinforcement, and communication problems that complicated their efforts. On the other hand, the Japanese advanced relentlessly due to being adequately supplied and trained.

Through a series of guerrilla attacks and sabotage missions, the Allied forces attempted to halt the Japanese advance, but the Japanese quickly learned to exploit the strategies and started attacking civilian targets as well.

Local Burmese and Indian soldiers were also enlisted by the Japanese forces under the promise of independence and freedom from British colonial rule. Although this tactic was successful in winning local support and demoralising the British forces, it also stoked fierce racial tensions and conflicts between the various groups.

CHAPTER XVII: TURNING OF THE TIDES

May 1942 brought with it an eventual halt to Japanese progress in the Pacific. The previous six months had radically changed the region's map with thousands of acres and formally sovereign lands under control of the Japanese Empire. However now the USA had managed to rebuild swaths of her naval fleet to compete at sea with the Japanese. Yamamoto's prediction was about to be put to the test.

THE BATTLE OF THE CORAL SEA

The Imperial Japanese Navy and the Allied forces, led by the United States and Australia, engaged in a crucial naval battle known as the Battle of the Coral Sea in May, 1942. Between the 4th and the 8th of the month, the battle took place in the Coral Sea, off the north-eastern coast of Australia.

The Japanese had recently captured several strategic locations in the Pacific, including the Philippines, Guam, Wake Island, and most importantly, Port Moresby in New Guinea. The capture and consolidation of Port Moresby would have eventually given the Japanese a base to launch further attacks on Australia, and potentially open up a route to invade the mainland.

Recognizing the significance of Port Moresby, the Allies made the decision to launch a counterattack in order to halt the Japanese advance. Two aircraft carriers, the USS Yorktown and USS Lexington, as well as a number of cruisers and destroyers were sent to intercept the Japanese fleet as part of a task force commanded by Admiral Frank J. Fletcher.

Both sides started their aerial searches for one another on May 4. When the Japanese aircraft spotted the US oiler Neosho and her escorting destroyer USS Sims, they launched an attack. The USS Sims was sunk, whereas the Neosho sustained significant damage before being scuttled. The Japanese, however, were unable to locate the US carriers.

The next day, May 5, the Japanese fleet, consisting of two carriers, the Shokaku and the Zuikaku, as well as several cruisers and destroyers, launched an attack on the Allied fleet. The Japanese had hoped to surprise the Allied forces and destroy their carriers, but the attack was detected by Allied aircraft, and the US carriers were able to launch their planes to intercept the Japanese.

The ensuing battle was fought entirely by aircraft, as both sides launched wave after wave of planes to attack each other's carriers. The Japanese aircraft were able to inflict serious damage on the USS Lexington, which was hit by several bombs and torpedoes and eventually sank. The Japanese also suffered heavy losses, with the Shokaku and the Zuikaku both sustaining significant damage.

On May 7, the Japanese fleet withdrew, believing that they had achieved their objective of preventing the Allied forces from reaching Port Moresby. In reality, the battle had prevented the Japanese from launching an invasion of Port Moresby, and it had weakened their naval power in the Pacific.

The Battle of the Coral Sea was the first naval conflict in history in which the opposing fleets relied solely on their aircraft to fight instead of engaging in direct combat. The fight was important because it kept the Japanese from colonising the Pacific and possibly invading Australia.

The battle was a costly one for both sides, with the USS Lexington sunk and the Japanese carriers badly damaged. However, it was a strategic victory for the Allies, as it marked the first time they had been able to halt the Japanese advance in the Pacific.

THE BATTLE OF MIDWAY

Between June 4 and June 7, 1942, off the coast of the island of Midway, the American and Japanese forces would once more clash. Strategically, Japan needed to take control of this checkpoint before launching a full-scale invasion of Hawaii. The majority of the US Pacific naval force would then be completely under Japanese control. It was crucial that the Americans maintain control of Midway as a result.

The American navy was clearly outmatched by the Japanese navy as the battle got underway. They outnumbered them, had better training, and had more cutting-edge technology. To take over the central Pacific, the Japanese intended to attack the American base on Midway Island.

American intelligence was aware of the Japanese plans because they were able to intercept Japanese communications. In order to confront the Japanese, the Americans had sent out their own fleet, and they had a secret weapon: the capacity to decipher Japanese codes.

The Japanese started attacking Midway Island on June 4. But as soon as they arrived, American aircraft launched a swift counterattack. Within the first few minutes of the battle, American planes were able to sink three Japanese aircraft carriers, severely wounding the Japanese navy.

Despite the initial success, the Americans were still outnumbered, and the battle raged on. The Japanese continued to launch attacks, but the Americans were able to hold their ground.

The turning point of the battle came when the Japanese launched a final, desperate attack on the American fleet.

The Japanese had planned to launch a massive assault with their remaining aircraft, but the Americans had anticipated this move. They had positioned their planes in such a way that they could easily intercept the Japanese planes as they approached.

American aircraft swooped down and engaged the Japanese aircraft in a dogfight, creating a dramatic scene. The roar of engines, the crackle of gunfire, and the cries of dying men filled the skies. Having downed most of the Japanese aircraft, the Americans ultimately prevailed.

The Americans achieved a significant victory at the Battle of Midway. They had been able to significantly damage the Japanese navy and turn the tide of the Pacific War. As the American offensive against Japan got underway, the battle signalled the end of Japanese territorial expansion in the Pacific.

THE ISLAND HOPPING CAMPAIGN

The Allies had to make a tough choice as World War II raged on in both Europe and the Pacific. The Allies needed a plan to retake these areas because the Japanese had taken over much of Southeast Asia and the Pacific. The solution was to launch an island hopping campaign, a plan that would eventually lead to the end of the war in the Pacific.

The strategy was designed to take advantage of the vast expanse of the Pacific Ocean. The Allies knew that the Japanese would be unable to defend every island in the Pacific, so they decided to bypass heavily fortified islands and focus on capturing less-defended ones. This would allow them to create a chain of bases that could be used to launch further attacks.

The first step in the island hopping campaign was the capture of Guadalcanal, a small island in the Solomon Islands chain. The campaign began with a surprise attack by the Allied forces, primarily consisting of the United States Marines, on the island of Guadalcanal in the Solomon Islands chain.

The objective of the mission was to secure the island and its airfield, which could be used as a strategic base for further attacks in the Pacific.

The sudden Allied assault caught the Japanese off guard because they had already established a significant presence on the island, including a sizable garrison and airfield. After a successful initial landing, the Japanese quickly launched a counterattack, sparking the start of the Guadalcanal battle.

The Japanese, who were determined to retake the island, engaged in intense combat with the Allied forces for several months. The Japanese launched a number of night time assaults on Allied positions, sneaking behind enemy lines and wreaking havoc.

One of the hardest battles of the entire conflict was the one for Guadalcanal. Both sides experienced illness and disease on the hot, humid island. The Japanese were adept at utilising the terrain to their advantage, and the Allies struggled to keep their supply routes open.

Nevertheless, despite the difficulties, the Allies were able to hold onto the island. The Japanese were eventually forced to withdraw their troops after they received supplies and additional reinforcements.

But the campaign did suffer some setbacks. Over 7,000 men were lost or injured for the Allies during the six-month conflict, resulting in significant casualties. With over 20,000 soldiers killed or missing in action, the Japanese suffered even greater losses.

A crucial turning point in the Pacific War was the Guadalcanal Campaign. The Allies' island-hopping strategy got its start with this, the first time the Japanese were routed on the ground. Both the Allied and Japanese forces experienced significant drops in morale as a result of the campaign.

Once they had Guadalcanal under their control, the Allies turned their attention to the Gilbert Islands' Island of Betio, which is a part of the Tarawa Atoll. Securing the island and its airfield, which could be used as a strategic base for additional attacks in the Pacific, was the mission's goal.

The island was heavily fortified by the Japanese with a web of bunkers, pillboxes, and trenches, making it a challenging target for the Allies.

Heavy naval bombardment of the island preceded the American assault, but the Japanese defences stood their ground. On November 20, 1943, 18,000 Marines descended on the beaches of Betio to begin the assault on the actual island.

The landing was met with strong resistance from the Japanese defenders, who had prepared well for the invasion. The Marines struggled to make headway against the Japanese defences, facing heavy machine-gun fire, mortars, and artillery.

Hand-to-hand combat was used in some of the fiercest and most intense battles. The shallow waters surrounding the island made it difficult for the Marines to land their supplies and heavy equipment.

The Marines were able to take control of the island in spite of these challenges. They engaged in combat as they moved inland, capturing bunker after bunker.

However, the conflict was far from over. Fighting lasted for several days as the Japanese kept launching unyielding counterattacks.

On November 23, the battle was declared over when the American flag was raised on Betio. The cost of the victory, however, was high. Over 3,000 casualties, including over 1,000 combat fatalities, were sustained by the Marines. Over 4,700 soldiers were lost for the Japanese army, making their losses even worse.

The Northern Mariana Islands' Island of Saipan was the next to be freed by the USA from Japanese rule. The Japanese used this as yet another strategic base from which to attack the US Pacific Fleet.

The conflict started on June 15, 1944, when the US launched a significant amphibious assault on the island. The Japanese defenders, who had heavily fortified the island, put up strong resistance to the American forces, which numbered over 71,000 men.

The American forces fought valiantly during the opening days of the battle to take control of the beaches and gain a foothold on the island. However, the Japanese defenders were ready and launched a number of counterattacks against the American forces.

Both sides suffered significant casualties as a result of the brutal and intense fighting. The difficult terrain made it difficult for the American forces to advance, and the Japanese defenders could hide in a number of hidden bunkers and caves.

Despite these challenges, the American troops were able to advance and gradually drive the Japanese defenders back. By July 7, American forces had taken control of the entire island and had routed the Japanese army.

The conflict on Saipan was noteworthy because it was the first time that Japanese civilians had been actively engaged in combat. Many Japanese civilians chose suicide over surrendering to American forces because the Japanese government had encouraged them to take up arms and fight alongside the military.

The American forces arrived in Guam in the Mariana Islands later that month, on July 21. The operation's goal was to take the island and establish a base for American forces to use to attack Japan.

In the battle, more than 50,000 American soldiers fought against about 20,000 Japanese defenders. Since the Japanese were well-defended on the island, the Americans encountered fierce resistance.

The American forces fought valiantly during the opening days of the battle to take control of the beaches and gain a foothold on the island. However, the Japanese defenders were ready and launched a number of counterattacks against the American forces.

Despite the tough resistance from the Japanese, the American forces managed to make steady progress and push deeper into the island. The fighting was brutal and intense, with both sides suffering heavy casualties. The Americans were hampered by the rugged terrain and the presence of many hidden bunkers and caves where the Japanese defenders could take cover.

As the battle progressed, the American forces managed to gain ground and slowly pushed the Japanese defenders back. The Japanese launched several counterattacks, but they were unable to regain control of the island.

Guam's battle was noteworthy because it was the first time American forces had reclaimed a region that had been lost to Japan during the war. The victory at Guam significantly raised American spirits and showed the military's strength in the face of unyielding resistance.

The battle of Peleliu was fought between September and November of 1944, following a brief interval of minor skirmishes and rearranging supplies and troops.

The battle kicked off with a ferocious naval bombardment intended to undermine the island's Japanese defences. The Japanese had created intricate tunnel systems and bunkers all over the island to shield them from the shelling, so the bombardment was largely ineffective. As a result, when the American forces arrived on the beaches of Peleliu, the Japanese defenders put up a strong fight.

The American troops found it difficult to advance due to Peleliu's rough terrain, which included steep hills and rocky terrain. The Japanese defenders employed a tactic of defending their positions at all costs, digging themselves into deep trenches and bunkers.

Some of the toughest and most exhausting fighting of the entire Pacific campaign took place on Peleliu. A highly skilled and determined foe who fought ferociously to defend every square inch of the island was in front of the American forces.

Despite the difficulties, the American forces were able to advance gradually, and they eventually succeeded in taking control of the island's airfield. However, this victory came at a high cost; the Japanese forces lost almost 10,000 people, while the American forces lost over 6,500.

Iwo Jima was seen as a necessary island to take over as the US drew closer to the Japanese mainland because it served as a base for Japanese fighter planes.

The Japanese forces, who had fortified the island with a vast network of tunnels, bunkers, and pillboxes, put up fierce resistance to the initial landing. The Americans came under heavy fire from Japanese machine guns and artillery, making the fighting brutal and intense.

Fighter planes would fly low over the battlefield and strafe Japanese positions with machine gun fire as part of a novel American strategy known as "close air support" during the battle. This strategy worked well because it compromised the Japanese defences and enabled the American troops to advance.

An iconic picture of American soldiers hoisting the American flag on Mount Suribachi, an island landmark, served as a reminder of the battle. The picture, which was taken by photographer Joe Rosenthal, became a representation of American triumph and tenacity.

Despite making progress, the Japanese continued to put up tremendous resistance, engaging in numerous suicide tactics like banzai charges and kamikaze attacks, and fighting to the death.

More than 6,000 American soldiers died in the conflict, and more than 18,000 were injured, making it one of the bloodiest battles of the Pacific War. Only 216 of the 21,000 defenders in the Japanese forces' forces managed to survive the battle, resulting in even greater losses.

On March 26, 1945, the conflict came to an end, with the Americans taking possession of the island. Iwo Jima's capture represented a significant victory for the Allies because it denied the Japanese a vital airbase and gave American bombers a strategic launching point for attacks on Japan.

One of Japan's largest non-mainland islands and the last stop on the island-hopping expedition was Okinawa. Securing Okinawa would cause a massive morale boost for the American forces and people back home.

The battle's aim was to seize Okinawa, an island in the Pacific strategically positioned between American and Japanese forces. The island was heavily fortified by the Japanese military with bunkers and tunnels and housed a sizable population of Japanese civilians.

American naval and aerial forces bombarded the island heavily before the battle even started. Following this, American troops arrived on the island and encountered ferocious Japanese defences. The Japanese used a strategy of defending their positions at all costs, frequently turning to suicide attacks, during the harsh and brutal fighting.

Okinawa has a challenging topography that makes it difficult for American forces to advance, including steep hills and cliffs, dense forests, and intricate networks of caves and tunnels. Because of their superior knowledge of the area and their skill and experience, the Japanese defenders launched unexpected attacks on the American forces.

As the conflict went on, both sides sustained significant losses. Along with the difficulty of navigating the island's rugged terrain, the possibility of Japanese counterattacks, and the overwhelming presence of civilians, the American forces encountered many difficulties.

Despite the difficulties, the American forces were able to advance gradually, and after 82 days of intense combat, they finally succeeded in taking the island. Although the American forces suffered more than 12,000 fatalities and 50,000 casualties, this victory came at a high cost. With more than 110,000 fatalities, the Japanese forces suffered even greater losses, including numerous civilians who were caught in the crossfire.

The Battle of Okinawa was significant because it was the final big battle of the Pacific campaign, and it showed how fiercely the Japanese defenders fought and how difficult the Pacific theatre was for American forces. As a result of the battle, thousands of innocent Okinawans lost their lives, underscoring the human cost of war.

The landscape of Japan after the war was significantly shaped by the Battle of Okinawa. The significant casualties suffered by the Japanese military and civilian population influenced the Japanese government's decision to submit to the Allied forces and end the war.

A problem had now arisen with the island hopping campaign. Although the US Naval fleet was on the cusp of Japan, the guerrilla warfare implemented by the Japanese soldiers had badly damaged the Americans. By the time the Japanese forces had surrendered, around 110,000 US personnel had died or were missing in the Pacific with a further 250,000 wounded.

With the War in Europe now won by the Allied forces, President Roosevelt needed a swift and decisive ending to the conflict in the Pacific. As fate would have it, July 1945 saw the first successful test of the very weapon that would change the Geopolitical landscape and warfare forever.

CHAPTER XVIII: THE MANHATTAN PROJECT

Cast your mind back to 1941 and the height of WW2. The war was raging on two fronts, in Europe and in the Pacific, and the US needed a weapon that could bring the conflict to a swift end. It was this sense of urgency that led to the creation of the Manhattan Project, a top-secret research initiative that would change the course of history.

The project was initiated in 1939, after Albert Einstein wrote a letter to President Franklin D. Roosevelt, warning him of the potential dangers of Nazi Germany developing an atomic bomb. At the time, the US had no idea how to develop such a weapon, but with Einstein's letter as a catalyst, Roosevelt authorised the creation of the Manhattan Project.

The Army Corps of Engineers division tasked with project management, the Manhattan Engineer District, inspired the project's name.

Although the project's initial budget was only $6,000, it eventually spiralled to an astounding $2 billion.

The man put in charge of the project was General Leslie R. Groves, a highly respected military engineer who was known for his organisational skills. Groves was given complete authority over the project, and he immediately began assembling a team of the best scientists and engineers in the country.

Robert Oppenheimer, a brilliant physicist who was put in charge of the scientific effort to develop the atomic bomb, was one of the key figures in the Manhattan Project. The task of designing the bomb and supervising the construction of the facilities required to develop it fell to Oppenheimer.

Enrico Fermi, an Italian physicist who had previously won the Nobel Prize for his work in nuclear physics, was a significant player in the project as well. The first nuclear reactor, which was used to make the plutonium required for the bomb, was developed in large part thanks to Fermi.

The Manhattan Project would develop over the coming years into the biggest engineering and scientific undertaking in history. The project would involve more than 130,000 people, including some of the brightest minds of the time.

The US required a weapon that could end the war, and this was the clear motivation behind the project. The ability of the atomic bomb to wipe out entire cities in a single blast made it the ideal tool for accomplishing this objective.

As the Manhattan Project continued to gain momentum, it became clear that there were a number of significant problems that needed to be overcome in order to successfully develop the atomic bomb.

One of the biggest challenges was finding a way to produce the necessary amount of fissile material, specifically plutonium. This required the construction of large-scale production facilities, which was a monumental task in itself. The facilities had to be constructed quickly and in secret, and they had to be designed to handle dangerous and highly radioactive materials.

The hiring and management of the large team of scientists and engineers working on the project was another significant problem. The scientists came from a variety of backgrounds and frequently approached problems in very different ways. It was difficult to lead and manage such a diverse group of people, and it called for excellent management and leadership abilities.

The size of the project itself, though, was possibly the biggest issue. There were no plans or precedents for the Manhattan Project, which was an unprecedented undertaking. Everything, from the design of the bomb to the production facilities to the safety protocols and procedures, had to be created by the scientists and engineers involved.

Additionally, this lack of precedent brought about a number of technical difficulties. To handle radioactive materials, for instance, or to test and improve the design of the bomb, the scientists had to create new theories and techniques. All of this required a great deal of experimentation, as well as significant trial and error.

As the project progressed, new challenges continued to emerge. There were numerous accidents and incidents involving radiation exposure, for example, which led to serious health problems for some of the workers involved. The construction of the production facilities also faced a number of setbacks, including issues with the availability of resources and delays caused by construction problems.

In addition to the project's logistical and technical difficulties, ethical questions also arose. The potential applications of the atomic bomb caused great internal conflict in many of the scientists working on the Manhattan Project; some even advocated for the project's complete cancellation. The ethical concerns only grew as the project progressed and it became clear that the bomb could potentially cause widespread destruction and loss of life.

THE FIRST SUCCESSFUL TEST

The first atomic bomb was successfully detonated on July 16, 1945, marking the Manhattan Project's successful completion of its primary objective.

The test, code-named "Trinity," was the result of years of work by the top scientists and engineers in the world, and it was conducted in the desert of Alamogordo, New Mexico.

The preparation for the test was rigorous. The scientists involved were aware that they were close to making a significant discovery, but there were also a lot of risks and unknowns. They had no idea how the bomb would actually behave or even if it would function at all.

The detonation itself was a magnificent sight. The bomb, which was mounted on a steel tower, was remotely detonated from a control bunker located a distance of several miles. A massive blast wave that shook the ground and launched debris into the air followed a blinding flash of light that illuminated the sky at the moment of detonation.

The engineers and scientists who had been working on the project for years observed the mushroom cloud rising into the sky in stunned silence. Although they were aware of the bomb's potential for power, they could not have predicted the explosion's sheer size.

The test was received with relief and triumph at first. The project's scientists overcame significant difficulties and hindrances, and the test's success served as proof of their perseverance and commitment.

There was, however, a feeling of dread and unease as well. The scientists were unsure of the long-term effects of their work even though they were aware that they had produced something incredibly destructive. The idea of using the bomb as a weapon of war caused serious doubt in the minds of some of them, and the possibility of utter devastation was never far from their thoughts.

News of the test quickly spread around the world, and it had a profound impact on the course of history. The Soviet Union, which had been working on its own atomic program, became aware of the test and began to fear the potential for nuclear war. The United States, meanwhile, saw the test as a major advantage in its ongoing conflict with Japan, and plans were quickly made to use the bomb as a weapon of war.

The Manhattan Project's successful atomic bomb test had a significant influence on the development of history.

It brought about a new era of warfare and technology that is still influencing the world today. However, it also brought up important ethical issues regarding the use of such a destructive weapon. The project's scientists were deeply conflicted about the implications of their work despite having accomplished a remarkable engineering and scientific innovation feat. The first successful test of the atomic bomb was a historic event, but it also altered the course of history.

Oppenheimer himself famously said, "Now I am becoming Death, the destroyer of worlds," after witnessing the first successful test of the bomb. It was clear that the world had entered a new era, one where the power to destroy entire cities lay in the hands of a select few.

The 4 year work of the scientists was completed. The news of the successful test was conveyed to President Truman by Secretary of War, Henry Stimson, in a private meeting at the White House.

Stimson briefed the President on the details of the test and the capabilities of the bomb, highlighting its immense destructive power. The President was initially taken aback by the news, recognizing the magnitude of the achievement and the potential implications for the future of warfare.

Despite his surprise, Truman remained composed and thoughtful, carefully considering the implications of the successful test. He was aware of the enormous risks and ethical concerns associated with the use of such a destructive weapon, and he recognized the need to weigh the potential benefits against the risks of using the bomb.

Roosevelt ultimately made the decision to proceed with the use of the atomic bomb as a weapon of war, believing that it was necessary to bring an end to the conflict with Japan and save American lives. The most destructive weapon in history at that point by a factor of 4,000 was ready to be deployed on the battlefield.

HIROSHIMA AND NAGASAKI

The world was forever altered when the United States dropped the first atomic bomb on the Japanese city of Hiroshima on August 6, 1945. The bomb was dropped by the Colonel Paul Tibbets-piloted B-29 bomber Enola Gay. Tibbets and his crew were prepared for the mission because they had spent months training for it and were aware of its significance and the seriousness of the situation.

The day began like any other, with residents going about their daily routines and preparing for work. At 8:15 am, a bright flash illuminated the sky over Hiroshima as the bomb, code-named "Little Boy," detonated with a deafening roar. In an instant, the city was plunged into chaos as buildings crumbled, fires broke out, and a massive mushroom cloud rose into the sky. The devastation caused by the bomb was unprecedented, and its impact was felt by the Japanese and the Americans alike.

Those who were closest to the explosion were killed instantly, while others were severely injured and disoriented. Survivors stumbled through the rubble, searching for loved ones and trying to make sense of what had just happened. The survivors had a difficult time adjusting to the bombing's effects as the city was left in ruins.

The response to the bombing in America was more conflicted. While some rejoiced over the mission's success and the end of the war, others were horrified by the damage the bomb had wrought. The decision to use the atomic bomb remains controversial to this day, with many questioning whether it was necessary to end the war and whether it was ethical to target civilians with such a devastating weapon.

Colonel Tibbets, who dropped the bomb on Hiroshima, was hailed as a hero by some and vilified by others. He believed that the mission was necessary to bring an end to the war as quickly as possible and prevent further casualties on both sides. However, he also acknowledged the devastation caused by the bomb and the impact it had on the people of Hiroshima.

Capt. Robert Lewis - second to Colonel Tibbets famously wrote in his log moments after seeing the bomb explode, "my God, what have we done."

After the bombing, the American military hailed Tibbets and his crew as heroes, and Tibbets received the Distinguished Service Cross for his contribution to the mission.

The Hiroshima attack is believed to have killed 66,000 people, and a further 69,000 were injured by radiation or debris. How many long-lasting health issues were brought on by the bomb's radiation is unknown.

The world was in shock following the horrific Hiroshima bombing. The first time the atomic bomb had ever been used, its destructive and horrific capabilities had been made clear. The world watched and waited in the days that followed to see how Japan would react to the bombing and whether the war would ultimately end.

The impact of the bomb left the Japanese government in disarray. Thousands of people had been killed or hurt, and the city of Hiroshima had been completely destroyed.

The Japanese military leaders, however, remained resolute and refused to submit to the Allied forces. Instead, they ordered the construction of more air-raid shelters to prepare for the possibility of additional bombings.

Meanwhile, the American military was preparing its next course of action. The US government decided that another bomb should be dropped on Japan in order to end the war, despite the devastation caused by the bombing of Hiroshima. A second bombing was already in the works, with several potential targets under consideration.

As the backup target for Hiroshima, Kokura, as well as Nagasaki and Niigata, were being considered, President Truman ordered the formation of a committee to choose the next target.

The American military started getting ready for the subsequent bombing as the committee debated the target. The bomb, code-named "Fat Man," was chosen to be carried by the B-29 bomber Bockscar, whose crew received intensive training for the mission.

On the island of Tinian, the bomb was brought, put together, and loaded onto the aircraft.

As tensions continued to escalate, the world waited anxiously to see what would happen next. On August 9, 1945, the Bockscar took off from Tinian and headed towards its target, Nagasaki.

At the time of the bombing, Nagasaki was a major industrial centre and home to many important military targets. Despite this, the city had been largely spared from air raids up until that point, and many of its citizens had no idea what was about to happen. In the early morning hours of August 9, the Bockscar approached the city and dropped the bomb, causing a massive explosion that could be seen from miles away.

The bombing's immediate aftermath was terrifying and chaotic. Much of the city was destroyed by the explosion, and in the hours and days that followed, wildfires raged throughout the city. Thousands of people died instantly, and thousands more were hurt or got stuck under the wreckage of the fallen structures.

The scale of the destruction brought on by the Nagasaki bombing was comparable to that of Hiroshima. Around 25,000 additional people experienced radiation sickness and other long-term health effects, bringing the total number of fatalities from the bombing's immediate aftermath to an estimated 40,000.

JAPAN SURRENDERS

The Japanese government was in disarray in the days following the bombings, with hardliners and moderates engaged in a savage debate over whether to pursue a negotiated settlement or continue hostilities. The Allies were also getting ready to launch a massive invasion of Japan that was expected to cause a great deal of casualties on both sides.

On August 9, the Soviet Union declared war on Japan and began a massive invasion of Manchuria, further weakening the already frail Japanese military. The situation reached a crisis point. The emperor Hirohito then addressed his people directly, pleading with them to accept the terms of the Allies' offer of surrender and calling for an end to the war.

The emperor's appeal was successful in ending the war despite the opposition of some hardliners within the military and government. Japanese officials and representatives of the Allies signed the formal surrender papers on August 14 aboard the USS Missouri in Tokyo Bay, putting an end to years of fighting and destruction.

World War II came to an end when Japan announced its total submission to the Allies on August 15, 1945. The announcement opened the door for a new era of international cooperation and peace after years of fierce fighting and devastating losses on both sides.

Numerous lives had been lost during the prolonged and vicious Pacific War, and entire cities had been levelled by the fighting. The conflict had been characterised by intense fighting and unfathomable hardship for all parties involved, from the surprise attack on Pearl Harbor to the bloody battles on the Pacific islands.

However, as the war came to an end, a new spirit of hope and tenacity started to emerge.

The war's events had permanently altered the world, and leaders from both sides realised that international politics and diplomacy required a new strategy.

The victory in the Pacific was the result of years of effort and sacrifice for the Allied powers. They had finally succeeded in defeating the Japanese Empire and putting an end to the war, which caused them to feel a great sense of pride and relief.

But for the people of Japan, the end of the war brought with it a sense of profound loss and devastation. The country had suffered tremendous losses in the fighting, with countless lives lost and entire cities destroyed. The surrender marked the beginning of a new era for Japan, one in which the country would have to rebuild and reimagine itself in the wake of the war's destruction.

THE IMPACTS OF WAR

This book has discussed the events of the war in Europe and the Pacific in terms of key figures, battles, geopolitics and global motivations. Whilst conveying the impact that WW2 had on the soldiers sent to fight across multiple nations and varying terrains, it has not mentioned in great detail the impact that the war had on the regular citizen.

Whether this be the French farmer who found his land occupied overnight, forced to give subsidies for the benefit and survival of the Third Reich or the shop owner in London whose business was levelled in a matter of seconds.

This section is to convey the impact that the deadliest conflict in history had on all of those who endured it.

CHAPTER XIX: THE HOLOCAUST

It was a moment that would be etched in the memories of the Allied soldiers forever. As they marched through the desolate landscape of Nazi Germany in the final days of World War II, they stumbled upon something unimaginable. A sight so horrific that it would leave them shaken to their core, and haunt them for the rest of their lives. They had discovered the Nazi death camps, and the atrocities committed within them.

As they cautiously approached the first camp, the soldiers could smell the stench of death and decay. The air was thick with the putrid smell of burning flesh, and the ground was littered with the bones of the countless victims who had perished there. The Allied soldiers were appalled by what they saw. They had heard rumours of the Nazi's treatment of Jews and other minorities, but nothing could have prepared them for the true horror of the Holocaust.

The soldiers wandered through the camp, taking in the sight of the emaciated bodies of the living and the dead. They saw the gas chambers, the ovens, and the piles of clothes and personal belongings that had once belonged to the victims. The Allied soldiers were overcome with a mix of rage and sorrow, and they knew that they had to do something.

As they continued to explore the camp, they encountered the survivors - those who had managed to cling to life despite the unimaginable horrors they had endured. The Allied soldiers were shocked at the sight of these survivors, and they did everything they could to help them. They gave them food and water, comforted them, and did their best to provide medical attention to those who needed it.

ROOTS OF THE HOLOCAUST

The Nazi regime's ideology was fundamental to the development of the Holocaust. The Nazi party, led by Adolf Hitler, had a clear agenda of racial dominance and superiority, with the aim of creating a so-called "Aryan" race.

They held the view that this race was the "most pure" race and that all other races were debased and unworthy of existence.

This ideology was fundamentally hateful of Jews, as well as other minorities like the Roma and Sinti, homosexuals, people with disabilities, and anyone who did not resemble their idealised version of the "perfect" Aryan race. The Nazi party held that Jews were the source of all evil in the world and were to blame for everything from political unrest to economic hardship.

Anti-Semitism was on the rise in Europe in the 1920s and 1930s, especially in Germany. Numerous factors, such as economic hardships, political unpredictability, and deeply ingrained anti-Semitic beliefs, contributed to this hatred of Jews.

Germany had fallen into chaos and economic turmoil following the conclusion of World War I. The fact that many Germans were having financial difficulties contributed to the growth of populist and nationalist movements.

These movements frequently used Jews as scapegoats for Germany's issues, accusing them of everything from political instability to economic hardships.

The treatment of Jews and other minorities drastically changed in the years right after Hitler came to power in Germany. Jews were increasingly the target of discrimination and violence as anti-Semitic policies became more common.

The Nazi party passed laws depriving Jews of their rights and property as one of its first acts after assuming power. They were barred from participating in certain occupations, attending particular institutions, and acquiring property. They were frequently the targets of violence and harassment in addition to being made to wear identifying symbols like the Star of David.

As the years passed, the situation for Jews in Germany grew more and more dire. The Nazi party was able to fire Jewish civil servants from their positions thanks to a law passed in 1933. A number of laws that forbade Jews from owning businesses, practising law or medicine, or even getting married to non-Jews followed this.

Dachau, a concentration camp in southern Germany not far from Munich, was the first to operate under the Nazi regime. Less than two months after Hitler was appointed Chancellor of Germany, it was founded in March 1933.

Initially built to house political prisoners, Dachau quickly devolved into a violent and terrifying place. Primarily Communists, Social Democrats, labour activists, and other political dissidents who were viewed as a threat to the Nazi party's hold on power comprised the majority of the prison's initial inmates.

From the start, the conditions in the camp were difficult. Prisoners endured torturous forced labour, brutal beatings, and other atrocities. They frequently went without food and medical attention, which caused widespread illness and death. Numerous people were subjected to cruel mistreatment, including medical experiments.

As the Nazi party's power grew, so too did the number of prisoners at Dachau. By the end of 1933, the camp held more than 4,000 inmates, including Jews, homosexuals, and other marginalised groups.

Dachau was also used as a training ground for the SS, the elite paramilitary unit of the Nazi party responsible for many of the most heinous crimes of the Holocaust. The SS used the camp as a laboratory for testing new methods of torture and interrogation, and many of its most notorious leaders got their start at Dachau.

On April 1, 1933, the Nazi party announced a nationwide boycott of Jewish-owned businesses in Germany. The boycott was advertised in the German media and posters were plastered across the country calling for Germans to avoid Jewish-owned businesses on April 1. The posters featured the message "Germans! Defend yourselves! Don't buy from Jews!"

The boycott was supported by the Nazi party, but also by various other organisations, including the German National People's Party and the National Socialist Women's League. These organisations encouraged their members to participate in the boycott, and many did so eagerly.

On the day of the boycott, many Germans did indeed avoid Jewish-owned businesses.

Some stores closed for the day, while others were vandalised by boycott supporters. Jewish store owners who attempted to open their businesses faced violence and intimidation, and many were forced to close permanently.

The boycott lasted for just one day, but its impact was far-reaching. It sent a clear message to the Jewish population in Germany that they were not welcome and that their businesses and livelihoods were at risk. It also emboldened the Nazi party and its supporters, who would go on to enact even more extreme anti-Semitic policies in the years to come.

On May 10th, 1933, students across Germany gathered to participate in a mass book burning organised by the Nazi party. The event was part of a larger campaign to rid Germany of so-called "un-German" literature, which included books written by Jewish authors, works critical of the Nazi party, and those deemed immoral or decadent. Nazi officials gave speeches criticising the books' authors and ideas while audiences applauded and sang national anthems.

The book burnings were a highly symbolic act, meant to demonstrate the Nazi party's commitment to censorship and the suppression of dissent. In the weeks leading up to the event, propaganda posters were plastered across Germany, encouraging citizens to turn in books for burning and warning of the dangers of "Jewish intellectualism."

The Nuremberg Laws, a set of laws intended to further marginalise and discriminate against Jews in Germany, were introduced by the Nazi party in September 1935. These laws, which were introduced at the annual meeting of the Nazi party in Nuremberg, had a significant impact on Germany's Jewish population.

The Law for the Protection of German Blood and German Honour was the initial Nuremberg Law. Due to this law, it was forbidden for Jews and non-Jewish Germans to get married or engage in sexual activity. Additionally, it forbade Jews from hiring Germans under the age of 45 as domestic workers if they were not Jewish. The penalties for breaking this law included imprisonment or forced labour.

The Reich Citizenship Law, the second law, deprived Jews of their German citizenship and converted them into subjects of the state. Furthermore, it denied Jews basic civil rights like the ability to vote and the right to own property, as well as the ability to hold military or public office.

The Jewish community in Germany was immediately impacted by the Nuremberg Laws. Jews had to wear distinguishing symbols like the yellow Star of David and were increasingly the targets of violence and harassment. Numerous Jews made an effort to leave the country, but were unsuccessful due to stringent immigration laws and the start of World War II.

Another important aspect of the Nuremberg Laws was that they established a legal framework for the persecution of Jews in Germany. They set the stage for even more extreme measures to follow, like the implementation of ghettos and concentration camps, and signalled the start of a concerted effort to marginalise and discriminate against Jews.

The international community responded to the Nuremberg Laws with shock and condemnation. Many countries, including the United States, implemented economic sanctions against Germany in protest. However, these measures were not enough to stop the Nazi party's anti-Semitic agenda, and the situation for Jews in Germany continued to deteriorate.

A turning point in the history of the Holocaust was the adoption of the Nuremberg Laws. They set the stage for the systematic persecution and extermination of millions of Jews and other minorities in Europe and represented a legal codification of the anti-Semitic ideologies of the Nazi party.

Hitler's armies entered Austria in March 1938 and proclaimed the end of the nation's independence. The Anschluss, an incident that marked a significant uptick in Nazi aggression, opened the door for even worse atrocities in the years to come.

As the Nazis established their dominance in Austria, they started to ruthlessly target the nation's Jewish population.

Jews were beaten and detained in the streets, synagogues were set on fire, and businesses were seized. Many people were compelled to leave their homes and look for safety in neighbouring nations.

With the signing of the Munich Agreement in September 1938, the situation deteriorated further. The Munich Agreement was a fatal blow to Jews living in Czechoslovakia. Their nation was essentially defenceless against the threat of the Nazis without the Sudetenland. As a result of the sharp increase in anti-Semitic violence, tens of thousands of Jews were detained and sent to concentration camps.

Jewish communities across Europe mobilised as the situation worsened in an effort to aid those who were fleeing persecution. While Zionist organisations worked to secure visas and secure safe passage to Palestine, organisations like the American Jewish Joint Distribution Committee offered assistance and support to refugees.

On the evening of November 9, 1938, riots broke out throughout Germany. It was the epoch-making night of Kristallnacht, also known as the Night of Broken Glass.

The events of that evening would be a turning point in the persecution of Jews by the Nazi regime.

After a young Jewish man killed a German diplomat in Paris, the violence started. The assassination served as a pretext for the Nazi leadership to incite anti-Semitic sentiment among the German populace. They demanded a "spontaneous demonstration" against the Jewish community, and it was met with an immediate and violent response.

Synagogues were demolished, Jewish-owned businesses were destroyed, and thousands of Jews were detained and sent to concentration camps throughout Germany. Berlin experienced particularly severe violence, leaving entire streets in ruins.

The destruction was not limited to Germany, however. In Austria, where the Anschluss had taken place only months before, Jewish homes and businesses were ransacked and destroyed. In total, it is estimated that more than 7,000 Jewish-owned businesses were destroyed during Kristallnacht, and at least 91 Jews were killed.

The violence of Kristallnacht was not limited to physical destruction. The Nazi regime also implemented a series of legal measures designed to isolate and dehumanise the Jewish community. Jewish children were expelled from schools, and Jews were prohibited from owning pets or even bicycles.

The international community reacted with shock and horror to the events of Kristallnacht. Many countries condemned the violence and pledged to take in Jewish refugees. However, for many Jews, it was already too late. They had lost everything and were left with no choice but to flee the country.

By 1939, more than 300,000 Jews had fled Germany and Austria, many of them forced to leave behind everything they owned. Many countries, including the United States, Canada, and Britain, were reluctant to accept Jewish refugees, citing concerns about immigration quotas and national security.

THE HOLOCAUST IN THE EARLY YEARS OF WW2

The treatment of Jews in Nazi-occupied areas drastically deteriorated as World War II got underway. Although the Nazi regime had long been committed to eradicating all Jews, the outbreak of war gave them new opportunities to carry out their genocidal plans.

The Nazi leadership implemented a policy of forced labour for Jewish men and women in the early stages of the war. Many of these Jews were sent to work in factories and other labour camps in harsh conditions with little regard for their health or well-being. Jewish people were denied their rights and freedoms while being used as cheap labour for the war effort under this policy.

In Polish cities like Warsaw, Lodz, and Krakow, the Nazis established a network of ghettos where they interned Jews and other targeted groups like Romani people and homosexuals. The ghettos were typically enclosed by high walls or barbed wire fences and were frequently found in the poorest, most congested areas of the cities. Jews had to endure living in small, unhygienic quarters with limited access to food, water, and medical care.

Poverty, hunger, and illness were a part of daily life in the ghettos. Many Jews were made to work long hours for little or no pay in factories or other workplaces. Because of the frequently unhygienic living conditions and inadequate medical care, disease outbreaks occurred in the ghettos. In the ghettos, thousands of people perished from starvation, illness, and other forms of abuse.

Numerous Jews in the ghettos rebelled against the Nazi government despite the appalling conditions they endured. Jews and their allies participated in sabotage, smuggling, and other forms of resistance as resistance movements arose in ghettos across Europe. In the Warsaw Ghetto, for example, Jewish resistance fighters staged an armed uprising against the Nazis in 1943, holding out for nearly a month before the ghetto was finally crushed.

The construction of Auschwitz began in 1940. This Nazi concentration and extermination camp was the biggest and most notorious, and it serves as a sombre reminder of the extent of human cruelty and suffering.

The location for the camp was selected in southern Poland, close to the town of Oswiecim, a region that already had a sizable Jewish population.

Beginning in May 1940, the camp's initial construction was carried out by prisoners who had been brought in from work camps and jails nearby. The camp was initially constructed using pre-existing structures, such as a former Polish army barracks that was quickly transformed into improvised jail cells.

But as the Nazi government stepped up its persecution of Jews and other minorities, it became clear that a bigger and more long-lasting camp was needed. Plans were made to build a new camp, which would later be known as Auschwitz II-Birkenau, in the summer of 1941.

Birkenau's construction was a significant undertaking. Prisoners from all over Europe were brought in to complete the work, and they were made to labour under appalling circumstances, frequently going without adequate food or shelter. The camp was constructed using prefabricated wooden huts that the prisoners put together on-site.

The existing camp at Auschwitz I was expanded and reorganised as Birkenau was being built. New structures were constructed, including a gas chamber and crematorium that were used to execute prisoners and Jews in bulk.

Extreme brutality and violence were evident during Auschwitz's construction. Inmates who were too ill or frail to work were put to death, and those who made an attempt at escapology were summarily executed. The prisoners in the camp endured unspeakably cruel conditions, including starvation, disease, and torture.

The prisoners who helped build the camp were determined to survive despite the horrific conditions. They created close-knit communities and elaborate survival techniques, frequently at great personal risk.

THE FINAL SOLUTION

On January 20, 1942, fifteen senior German officials gathered at a villa in the Berlin suburb of Wannsee to discuss the implementation of the "Final Solution," the Nazi plan to exterminate the Jewish population of Europe.

The meeting was chaired by Reinhard Heydrich, head of the Reich Security Main Office and one of the key architects of the Holocaust.

The Wannsee Conference was a turning point in the history of the Holocaust. Until that time, the mass murder of Jews had been carried out in an ad hoc and decentralised manner, with different agencies and departments responsible for various aspects of the killing process. The purpose of the conference was to coordinate the various agencies and to establish a clear and efficient plan for the systematic murder of all European Jews.

The participants at the Wannsee Conference included representatives from the SS, the Gestapo, the Foreign Ministry, and various other government agencies. Heydrich opened the conference by stating that the "Final Solution" had been authorised by Adolf Hitler and that its goal was the "total solution of the Jewish question in Europe."

The main agenda item at the conference was the identification and deportation of Jews from across Europe to extermination camps in occupied Poland.

Heydrich estimated that there were approximately 11 million Jews living in Europe, of which about half were in the territories under German control. He outlined a plan to concentrate the Jewish population of Europe in ghettos and labour camps, and then to transport them to extermination camps in the east for systematic murder in gas chambers.

The conference was marked by a cold and bureaucratic tone, with the participants referring to the Jews as "evacuees" and "special treatment cases." Heydrich emphasised the importance of secrecy and security, warning the participants that the "Jewish question" was one of the most sensitive and delicate issues facing the German government.

The Wannsee Conference was a gathering to coordinate the implementation of already established policies rather than a decision-making body. Although it signalled a change from ad hoc measures to an organised and systematic genocide, it also provided a clear and explicit statement of the Nazi plan for the "Final Solution."

Early in March of that year, special mobile killing squads known as Einsatzgruppen carried out the first murders. Other "undesirables" like Roma, homosexuals, and political dissidents were also to be rounded up and put to death by these units.

The killings took place in Soviet Union regions that had previously been occupied by Nazi forces during Operation Barbarossa. All Jews and other local "enemies of the state" would be rounded up by the Einsatzgruppen as they moved from town to town. Then, after forcing them to dig their own mass graves in nearby fields or forests, they would march them there, shoot them, and bury them in those graves.

The Einsatzgruppen employed brutal and horrifying techniques. Before being shot, many of the victims were made to strip naked, and the bodies were frequently left out in the open for days or even weeks before being buried. Additionally, the Einsatzgruppen frequently used local accomplices to help with the killings, which only increased the horror.

In addition to the Einsatzgruppen, the Nazis also ramped up the construction of concentration camps in 1942. These were initially intended to be places where Jews and other "enemies of the state" could be held before being sent to the death camps. However, the conditions in these camps were so harsh that many prisoners died from disease, starvation, or overwork.

The scale of the killings that took place in 1942 was staggering. It is estimated that between March and December of that year, the Einsatzgruppen alone were responsible for the deaths of around 1.4 million Jews and other "enemies of the state." When combined with the deaths in the concentration camps, the total number of Jewish victims during this period is estimated to be around 2 million.

In 1943, the Holocaust was in full swing. The events of this year were marked by a number of significant developments, including mass deportations, uprisings in ghettos and concentration camps, and the implementation of new methods of killing.

The Warsaw Ghetto's destruction was one of the year's most important events. The ghetto had been occupied by the Nazis for three years at this point, during which time its residents had endured starvation, disease, and ongoing terror. The Nazis started transporting thousands of Jews from the ghetto to the Treblinka concentration camp in January of that year. Jewish fighters formed a resistance movement as the deportations went on, determined to retaliate against their oppressors.

The Nazis started the final phase of the Warsaw Ghetto's destruction on April 19, 1943. The Jewish fighters attacked Nazi positions all over the ghetto with their arsenal of weapons and homemade explosives. They held off the Nazi forces for nearly a month, despite being vastly outnumbered and outgunned, until the last resistance fighters were captured or killed. Jewish tenacity and resistance in the face of Nazi brutality were represented by the Warsaw Ghetto Uprising.

The killing, meanwhile, went on nonstop in the concentration camps. The Nazis started mass murdering prisoners in gas chambers at Auschwitz, the largest and most notorious of the camps.

Large numbers of prisoners were herded into gas chambers and killed with poisonous gas in an orderly and effective manner.

Some prisoners in the camps managed to put together their own resistance movements despite the appalling conditions and constant threat of death. A group of Jewish inmates at Sobibor succeeded in breaking out of the camp, killing several Nazi guards in the process. The majority of them were eventually apprehended and killed, but the escape was a stark reminder of the prisoners' resolve to fight back against their oppressors.

With victories in North Africa and the Soviet Union, the Allies advanced in the war throughout 1943. However, they mostly failed in their attempts to stop the Holocaust. Tens of thousands of Jews were able to be moved to safety in impartial Switzerland in August thanks to a deal that a group of Jewish leaders from Slovakia were able to broker with the Nazis. Even though this was a rare success, it wasn't nearly enough to stop the Holocaust from spreading.

The Holocaust changed course in 1944 when the Nazis stepped up their efforts to wipe out all of Europe's Jews. The war was now moving against Germany, but Hitler was adamant that his genocidal scheme would be carried out to the bitter end.

Deporting Jews from Hungary was one of the most important events of 1944. Hungary had been a German ally, and up until this point, the approximately 800,000 Jews living there had largely been spared. However, German troops occupied Hungary in March 1944, and the deportation of its Jews started soon after.

The Nazis used deceptive tactics to convince the Hungarian Jews to comply with the deportations, including telling them that they were being resettled to work camps rather than death camps. Trains filled with Jewish men, women, and children were sent to Auschwitz and other death camps, where the vast majority were murdered upon arrival.

Perhaps one of the most tragic events of the Holocaust took place in early 1945 with the Auschwitz Death March.

As the Allies were closing in on the Nazi concentration and extermination camps, the Nazis began to evacuate and move prisoners to other camps in order to cover up their crimes. One of the largest and most brutal of these forced marches was the evacuation of Auschwitz, which took place in the harsh winter of 1945.

On January 17, 1945, the evacuation of Auschwitz began. In total, over 60,000 prisoners were forced to leave the camp, including those who were too sick or weak to walk. The march was brutal, with prisoners enduring freezing temperatures, little food or water, and extreme exhaustion. Nazi guards were merciless, shooting anyone who couldn't keep up or who tried to escape.

The prisoners were forced to march for days, covering long distances on foot with no rest. Many died along the way, collapsing from exhaustion, starvation, and exposure to the bitter cold. The sick and weak were left behind to die, with no medical attention or care. Those who managed to survive the march arrived at other camps, where they were subjected to more brutal treatment.

The march itself was a horrific scene of suffering and death. The prisoners marched in columns, their emaciated bodies covered in rags and blankets. Many had no shoes or coats, and were forced to walk barefoot through the snow. The sounds of gunshots and the cries of the dying echoed through the forest as the march continued.

The conditions were so brutal that even the Nazi guards themselves began to falter. Many of them were also freezing, starving, and exhausted, and some were unwilling to shoot prisoners who were unable to continue. As the march continued, some prisoners were able to escape, with the help of sympathetic civilians who offered them food, shelter, and warm clothes.

The Auschwitz Death March continued for weeks, with prisoners enduring unimaginable suffering and brutality. By the time the survivors reached their destinations, they were barely alive, with many dying shortly after their arrival. The death toll of the march is unknown, but estimates suggest that tens of thousands of prisoners died along the way.

LIBERATION

The conclusion of World War II had a significant effect on the Jewish community, especially on those who had survived the horrors of the Holocaust. Europe had been destroyed by the war, and millions of people were forced to flee, become homeless, and struggle to start over.

The end of the war brought a range of emotions, including relief, grief, and uncertainty, for many Jewish survivors. The Holocaust and the Nazi regime's downfall were heralded by the end of the war, but it also meant that millions of Jews had been killed, and those who were left faced the daunting task of rebuilding their lives in a world that had been irrevocably altered by the war.

In the immediate aftermath of the war, many Jewish survivors found themselves living in Displaced Persons (DP) camps set up by the Allied forces. These camps were often overcrowded and lacked basic necessities, and the survivors had to deal with the trauma of their experiences in the concentration camps.

For many, the end of the war also meant a search for surviving family members. After years of separation and uncertainty, survivors were desperate to find their loved ones and reunite with them. However, the search was often futile, as many families had been torn apart and scattered throughout Europe.

Jewish survivors experienced a wave of immigration after the war. Many people wanted to emigrate from Europe and begin new lives in Israel or somewhere else in the world. Those who remained had a difficult time rebuilding their lives because they had to deal with the trauma of their experiences and the difficulties of reintegrating into society.

In the years following the war, many Jewish survivors became involved in the Zionist movement, which aimed to establish a Jewish homeland in Palestine. This movement gained significant momentum in the wake of the Holocaust, as many Jews felt that they had nowhere else to turn to for safety and security.

Although it is difficult to pinpoint the precise number of deaths brought on by the Holocaust, estimates place the number of Jewish fatalities at about six million. This figure roughly corresponds to two-thirds of all Jews living in Europe at the time. Along with Jews, the Nazi regime also persecuted Romanis, homosexuals, people with disabilities, and other groups deemed undesirable. The Holocaust is thought to have killed anywhere between 11 and 17 million people in total.

One of the most infamous concentration camps was Auschwitz, located in Poland. Auschwitz was a complex of three main camps and 40 sub-camps, and it was responsible for the deaths of an estimated 1.1 million people, most of whom were Jews. Other notorious camps include Treblinka, which was responsible for the deaths of 800,000 people, and Belzec, which saw the murder of an estimated 600,000 people.

Numerous other people perished as a result of the circumstances they encountered while attempting to flee, in addition to those who were killed by the Nazis directly. Many Jews tried to emigrate to other nations, but the majority were turned away.

Some were apprehended and returned to their native countries, where they were executed or made to live in concentration camps or ghettos.

The Holocaust caused a staggering number of deaths, and its effects on the world are immeasurable. The trauma of this incident has been carried by the survivors and their offspring for many generations. The Holocaust serves as a poignant reminder of the perils of hatred and intolerance as well as the value of resisting oppression and discrimination.

CHAPTER XX: THE REFUGEE CRISIS

It was the height of World War II, and Europe was in chaos. People were fleeing their homes, seeking safety and security in far-off lands. The refugee crisis of World War II was one of the largest and most devastating in history, with millions of people displaced and uprooted from their homes. But what caused this crisis? How did it come about?

We must look back to the early stages of the war to comprehend the reasons behind the World War II refugee crisis. Invading Poland in September 1939, Germany started a series of events that ultimately resulted in the eviction of millions of people. People emigrated from their homes in search of safety as the war spread throughout Europe.

MINORITY GROUPS

As mentioned earlier, the Nazi regime's treatment of Jews, Romani people, homosexuals, and other minority groups was one of the main reasons for the refugee crisis.

The Nazis sought to exterminate those they considered to be inferior because they held the idea of a supposed "Master Race." As a result, ghettos and concentration camps were established, as well as laws like the Nuremberg Laws that deprived Jews of their rights and citizenship.

The Nazis stepped up their efforts to eradicate these groups as the war dragged on, which resulted in massive exterminations and deportations. Many people were forced to leave their homes as a result, frequently leaving behind everything they owned. Many non-Jewish Germans also left the country out of fear for their lives under the Nazi regime, in addition to Jews and other minorities.

The refugee crisis was a particularly terrifying experience for Jews, homosexuals and Romani people. Many people were taken against their will from their homes and taken to concentration and extermination camps, frequently leaving behind everything they owned. There, they endured cruel treatment, forced labour, and ultimately death.

Being a refugee was an equally traumatic experience for those who were able to flee. Many were forced to live in overcrowded refugee camps after fleeing to neighbouring countries, frequently with only the clothes on their backs. These camps commonly had terrible living conditions, with little access to food, water, or healthcare. Despite the difficulties, many were able to endure and start over in new nations.

Initially, the response to the refugee crisis was slow and ineffective. Many countries were reluctant to accept refugees, particularly those from minority groups, and imposed strict immigration quotas that made it difficult for refugees to gain entry. The United States, for example, had strict immigration laws that limited the number of refugees it would accept, and many other countries followed suit.

However, as the conflict continued, the international community started to act more actively to address the refugee crisis. To help refugees and advocate for their rights, groups like the International Red Cross and the United Nations High Commissioner for Refugees (UNHCR) were founded.

These organisations put in a lot of effort to provide food, shelter, and medical attention to refugees.

Additionally, many nations started to be more proactive in accepting refugees. For instance, many other nations eventually concurred with the United States to accept refugees from Europe. But many nations still imposed strict immigration quotas, making it challenging for refugees to enter.

The Kindertransport programme, which was established in the UK to provide safe passage for Jewish children from Germany and other nations, was one of the most notable responses to the refugee crisis. Nearly 10,000 kids were brought to the UK as part of the programme and placed with foster families or children's homes. Many Jewish families looked to the programme as a ray of hope because they saw it as a chance to protect their children from the atrocities of the Nazi regime.

Ultimately, however, the response to the refugee crisis was insufficient despite these efforts.

Numerous individuals were unable to flee the atrocities of the war, and millions of people were left without adequate protection or assistance. For minority groups, in particular, the response was often insufficient, with many countries reluctant to accept refugees from these groups.

ALLIED BOMBING CAMPAIGNS

There were many factors contributing to the refugee crisis brought on by Allied bombing campaigns. The size and ferocity of the bombing campaigns were a significant contributing factor. Millions of tonnes of bombs were dropped on Axis targets by Allied forces, levelling buildings, infrastructure, and entire cities. Many people were compelled to leave their homes in search of safety and shelter as a result.

Furthermore, the bombing campaigns frequently hit important transportation hubs, making it challenging for refugees to reach safety. It was challenging for people to flee the conflict zone because roads, bridges, and railways were frequently destroyed or damaged. Due to this, many refugees were forced to travel on foot or by other means, frequently risking their lives.

The indiscriminate nature of the bombing campaigns was another factor causing the refugee crisis. Even though the Allies made an effort to limit civilian casualties, the bombings still resulted in the deaths or injuries of numerous innocent people. The civilian population experienced a sense of fear and insecurity as a result, which exacerbated the refugee crisis.

The cost it took on those forced to flee their homes was one of the refugee crisis' most immediate effects. Many refugees were compelled to rely on the kindness of others in order to survive after being left without access to adequate food, shelter, or medical care. The result was a large population of hungry, ill, and suffering refugees.

Additionally, the large-scale population displacement had a significant impact on the economies and societies of the crisis-affected nations. Numerous refugees were unable to find employment or contribute to the economy, which had a detrimental effect on the nations that were hosting them. In many areas of Europe, this had a significant economic and social impact in addition to the damage caused by the bombings.

The refugee crisis also had a profound impact on international relations and the post-war world. The scale and scope of the crisis made it clear that governments and international organisations needed to take action to address the needs of refugees and other displaced persons. This led to the creation of the United Nations High Commissioner for Refugees (UNHCR) and other organisations dedicated to providing aid and support to refugees.

The refugee crisis also highlighted the need for greater international cooperation and understanding in the wake of the war. Many refugees were forced to flee across borders, leading to tensions and conflicts between nations over the issue of refugee resettlement. However, the crisis also led to greater cooperation between nations in addressing the needs of refugees, and set the stage for the international refugee policies that exist today.

Perhaps most importantly, the refugee crisis caused by Allied bombing campaigns was a stark reminder of the human cost of war. The suffering of the refugees, who were innocent victims of the conflict, was a testament to the need for peace and understanding between nations.

It was a reminder that the actions of governments and military forces can have profound consequences for civilian populations, and that the needs of refugees and other displaced persons must be taken into account in any conflict.

POLITICAL REFUGEES

Many people were displaced as a result of the political unrest and violence of World War II, including those who were persecuted for their political views and actions. Political refugees during and after the war encountered many difficulties while attempting to flee persecution and start over in new nations.

One of the most significant groups of political refugees during the war were those who opposed the Nazi regime in Germany and other Axis powers. These individuals often faced imprisonment, torture, and execution for their resistance activities, and many were forced to flee their homes and seek refuge elsewhere.

Many of these refugees still struggled to find safe havens and start new lives despite the establishment of political refugee camps and aid organisations like the International Red Cross.

Political refugees from nations occupied or ruled by the Axis powers were present alongside those escaping Nazi persecution. For instance, citizens of nations like Poland and Czechoslovakia who disagreed with the puppet governments put in place by Germany frequently had to flee their homes and look for safety in other nations. As they attempted to acclimatise to new societies and start new lives, these refugees faced particular difficulties, such as language barriers and cultural differences.

The end of the war did not bring an end to political persecution and displacement. In fact, the post-war period saw the rise of new political conflicts and tensions, particularly between Western powers and the Soviet Union. Many individuals who were seen as threats to the Soviet regime, including intellectuals, dissidents, and artists, were forced to flee their homes and seek refuge in Western countries.

These refugees often faced suspicion and discrimination, as their political beliefs and affiliations made them targets of surveillance and harassment.

The political and cultural landscapes of their new countries were greatly influenced by political refugees during and after World War II, despite the difficulties they faced. Many went on to become influential figures in their neighbourhoods who promoted social justice and human rights. Others made contributions to the sciences and arts, enhancing the national cultures of their adopted nations.

CHILD REFUGEES

During World War II, children who were refugees faced a variety of difficulties, including being cut off from their families, lacking access to healthcare and education, and being exposed to violence and trauma. As a result of German bombings, the most well-known group of child refugees during the war were those who were evacuated from cities in Britain and other Allies. The government made the decision to relocate millions of kids from urban areas to rural areas.

Over three million children were evacuated during the first few days alone, making the evacuation programme one of the largest mass movements of people in British history.

The evacuation procedure was a perplexing and distressing experience for many kids. Many of them were being separated from their families for the first time, and they were given little information about where they were going or how long they would be gone. Children as young as five years old waited in lines at train stations across the nation on the morning of September 1, 1939, with a gas mask around their neck, a small suitcase in their hands, and a label sewn to their clothes indicating their name, age, and destination.

Many children were also forced to leave their homes in other regions of Europe and Asia due to the war, especially those who were being persecuted due to their ethnicity or religion. Jewish children in particular were in grave danger because the Nazi regime wanted to exterminate them.

Despite the enormous hardships that child refugees endured both during and after World War II, many of them went on to significantly contribute to their adopted nations. Others devoted their lives to advocacy and social justice, while others rose to prominence in business, politics, and the arts.

GERMAN REFUGEES POST WAR

The aftermath of World War II saw a mass displacement of people across Europe, particularly in Germany. With the country devastated by the war, millions of Germans were forced to flee their homes in search of safety, food, and shelter.

Many Germans found themselves displaced within their own country, as the fighting had destroyed entire cities and left millions homeless. The government struggled to provide basic necessities like food and shelter, and many Germans had to resort to living in makeshift shelters or in bombed-out buildings.

Others were compelled to flee to nearby nations like Austria and Czechoslovakia out of fear of reprisals from the victorious Allies. These refugees had a challenging journey ahead of them, frequently walking for days or weeks on end with scant supplies and inadequate protection.

After World War II, how German refugees were treated varied greatly depending on where they were and how they were treated. The Allied forces and the citizens of the nations they fled to treated many Germans with suspicion and hostility.

German refugees have occasionally faced violence and harassment from locals who accuse them of starting the war. This was particularly true for Germans who fled to countries like Poland and Czechoslovakia, which had been occupied by Nazi Germany during the war.

Other times, German refugees received better care and consideration. Some Allied forces were sympathetic to the plight of the German people and made efforts to help and support the displaced.

Depending on the refugee's age and gender, different approaches were taken to them. Children and women were frequently considered to be less dangerous and were thus more likely to be accepted into new communities. Men were frequently subjected to greater hostility and suspicion, especially if they had served in the German military or were thought to be Nazis.

The post-war era was one of uncertainty and difficulty for many German refugees. Many people struggled to find enough food, shelter, and medical care because the country was in ruins. This was especially true for those who had to leave their homes and communities behind in order to start over somewhere else.

Despite the difficulties they encountered, many German refugees managed to rebuild their lives in the years following the war. Many of the refugees were able to assimilate into their new communities thanks to the government's assistance in helping them find new homes and jobs.

CHAPTER XXI: ROLE OF WOMEN

Men were required to enlist in the military and defend their nations as the world descended into World War II's chaos. But men were not the only ones fighting in this conflict. Both at home and in active combat, women from all over the world were essential to the war effort.

Women made numerous and diverse contributions to the war. Some worked in factories and offices to support the war effort, while others served in the military as nurses, pilots, or even combatants. The war gave many women the chance to reject conventional gender roles and establish themselves as valuable contributors to society.

WOMEN IN COMBAT

As nations mobilised their armies, it became evident that the war required the participation of all citizens, including women. With so many men being drafted into the military, women were called upon to step up and serve in various roles, including combat.

While women had served in auxiliary roles in previous conflicts, World War II marked the first time that women were allowed to enlist in the military as full-fledged members. In the United States, the Women's Army Corps (WAC) was established in 1942, providing an opportunity for women to serve in the military. Women were also recruited for other roles in the military, such as the Navy's Women Accepted for Volunteer Emergency Service (WAVES) and the Women Airforce Service Pilots (WASPs).

Women were conscripted into the military in the Soviet Union and served in a range of combat positions, such as snipers, pilots, and tank drivers. As an example, the 46th Taman Guards Night Bomber Aviation Regiment, which became well-known for its nocturnal bombing raids on German targets, was one of the Soviet Union's female-only units.

In Great Britain, women were recruited into the Women's Auxiliary Air Force (WAAF) and served in various roles, including air traffic controllers, radio operators, and mechanics. Women also served in the Special Operations Executive (SOE), a covert organisation that carried out sabotage and espionage missions behind enemy lines.

Although they were not permitted to serve in units that engaged in direct combat, women served in combat roles in the US as well. Women worked as support staff instead, such as mechanics, clerks, and nurses. With nurses providing vital medical care to injured soldiers on the front lines, the Army Nurse Corps played a particularly significant role in the war effort.

During World War II, women made valuable and significant contributions to combat. They paved the way for later generations of female soldiers who would continue to dismantle stereotypes and take on combat roles.

While the war had a profound impact on the role of women in society, it also highlighted the inequalities that women faced.

One of the primary issues that women faced in combat roles was discrimination. Many military leaders and soldiers believed that women were not suited for combat and should not be allowed to serve in direct combat units. This led to women being relegated to support roles, such as mechanics, clerks, and nurses.

Women in combat roles also faced physical challenges. Many women were not physically as strong as men, which made it difficult for them to carry heavy equipment and weapons. They also had to contend with the physical demands of combat, such as long marches, extreme weather conditions, and sleep deprivation.

Another issue that women faced in combat roles was the lack of proper equipment and training. Women often had to use equipment that was designed for men, which did not fit properly and made it difficult for them to carry out their duties. Women also received less training than their male counterparts, which put them at a disadvantage in combat situations.

Sexual harassment and assault were also major issues that women faced in combat roles. Women who reported incidents of harassment or assault were often met with disbelief or blamed for the incident. This created a hostile environment for women and made it difficult for them to report incidents and receive support.

Despite these challenges, women in combat roles continued to serve their country with bravery and dedication. Their contributions helped to pave the way for future generations of women in the military.

WOMEN ON THE HOME FRONT

One of the most significant contributions that women made on the home front was in the workforce. With so many men serving in the military, there was a shortage of labour in industries such as manufacturing, agriculture, and transportation. Women stepped in to fill these jobs, taking on roles that were traditionally reserved for men.

Many women who had previously been confined to the home or limited to low-paying jobs found new opportunities in the workforce.

They worked in factories, producing everything from aircraft to ammunition. They worked on farms, harvesting crops and raising livestock. They worked in offices, hospitals, and schools, providing critical support services to the war effort.

At first, many employers were hesitant to hire women for jobs traditionally held by men. They were concerned that women were not physically capable of handling the work or that they lacked the dedication and commitment of their male counterparts. However, as the war continued, it became clear that women were just as capable as men in the workforce. They proved themselves to be reliable, hardworking, and dedicated, often working long hours and making significant sacrifices to support the war effort.

Despite their contributions, women in the labour force faced numerous challenges and obstacles. They were often paid less than men for the same work and were denied opportunities for advancement. Many were subjected to harassment and discrimination, with employers and male co-workers questioning their abilities and commitment to the job.

Despite these challenges, women in the labour force remained committed to their work and the war effort. They proved themselves to be indispensable to the war effort, working tirelessly to produce the materials and goods needed to support the troops overseas. Their contributions helped to shape the course of the war and laid the groundwork for increased opportunities for women in the workforce in the years to come.

WOMEN IN ESPIONAGE AND RESISTANCE

Women played a critical role in resistance movements and spying efforts. From covert operations to open rebellion, women made significant contributions to the war effort, often at great personal risk.

One of the most prominent examples of women's involvement in resistance movements was the French Resistance. They gathered intelligence, disrupted supply lines, and provided aid to Allied forces. Women in the resistance were often targeted by Nazi forces, and many faced torture, imprisonment, or execution for their activities.

Women in the Resistance faced numerous challenges and dangers. They worked in secrecy, often separated from their families and communities. They risked arrest, torture, and execution for their activities, and many faced discrimination and scepticism from their male counterparts. Despite these obstacles, women continued to make significant contributions to the Resistance effort, using their intelligence, courage, and resourcefulness to support the Allied cause.

One of the most prominent female members of the French Resistance was Marie-Madeleine Fourcade. Fourcade was a young mother and a member of the French aristocracy who joined the Resistance in 1941.

She was appointed the head of Alliance, the largest Resistance network in France, and became one of the most wanted women in France by the Gestapo. Fourcade used her skills as a leader and organiser to coordinate Resistance activities and establish communication networks with Allied forces. She was eventually captured by the Gestapo and imprisoned, but she managed to escape and continue her work until the end of the war.

Another notable female member of the French Resistance was Lucie Aubrac. Aubrac was a schoolteacher who joined the Resistance with her husband, Raymond. The couple worked together to organise Resistance activities, including the rescue of Resistance leader Jean Moulin. Aubrac also worked as a courier, carrying messages and supplies between Resistance cells. She was eventually captured and imprisoned by the Gestapo but managed to escape with the help of her husband and fellow Resistance members.

Women in the French Resistance used a variety of tactics to support the Allied cause. They often worked as couriers, carrying messages and supplies between Resistance cells. They also disrupted Nazi supply lines by sabotaging railway lines, bridges, and communication networks. Women in the Resistance also played a crucial role in gathering intelligence, often using their status as women to gather information without arousing suspicion.

In addition to their role in resistance movements, women were also heavily involved in spying efforts.

Many women worked as intelligence agents, gathering vital information about enemy troop movements, weapons development, and strategic plans. Women were well-suited for this work, often able to blend in more easily in social situations and gather information without arousing suspicion. They used a variety of tactics, including codebreaking, clandestine meetings, and wiretapping, to gather information and relay it to Allied forces.

One of the most famous female spies of the war was Virginia Hall, an American who worked for the British Special Operations Executive (SOE). Hall worked undercover in France, gathering intelligence and coordinating resistance activities. Despite being targeted by the Gestapo, she managed to evade capture and continue her work until the end of the war. Hall's contributions to the war effort were so significant that she was awarded the Distinguished Service Cross by the United States government.

WOMEN IN OCCUPIED TERRITORIES

During World War II, women living in occupied territories faced tremendous challenges and hardships. They were subjected to the brutalities of war, including forced labour, rape, and torture. Many were separated from their families and communities and forced to live under the rule of foreign powers. Despite these difficulties, women in occupied territories showed remarkable resilience and strength, finding ways to resist and survive in the face of adversity.

Women were often forced to work for the occupying forces. This forced labour was a part of the Nazi policy of exploiting the occupied territories for the benefit of the German war machine. Women were subjected to long hours of work and were often treated brutally by their overseers.

In many cases, women were forced to work in factories, producing goods for the German war effort. The work was often dangerous and involved exposure to toxic chemicals and fumes.

Women were required to work long hours, with little or no breaks, and were often subject to harsh punishments for any mistakes or perceived slowness.

Other women were forced to work on farms, providing labour for the production of food for the German army. This work was also difficult and involved long hours of physical labour in all kinds of weather. Women were often required to work with little or no protection from the elements, and many suffered from malnutrition and disease.

In addition to the physical demands of forced labour, women in occupied territories were often subject to sexual exploitation and abuse by their overseers. Many women were forced to provide sexual services to the occupying soldiers, either through coercion or outright violence. Others were subjected to rape or other forms of sexual violence.

Many women were forced into sexual slavery, often referred to as "comfort women," and were used for the sexual gratification of German soldiers.

These women were typically taken from their homes or captured in raids, and were often subjected to brutal treatment, including physical abuse and torture.

The women who were forced into sexual slavery were subjected to a constant stream of sexual violence and abuse, often by multiple soldiers over a period of days or even weeks. They were provided with little or no food, clothing or medical care, and were often left to suffer from sexually transmitted diseases or other injuries.

For many women, the trauma of sexual exploitation continued long after the war had ended. Many were unable to return to their homes or communities due to the stigma of having been used as sexual objects by the occupying forces. Others suffered from physical or psychological scars that lasted a lifetime, including post-traumatic stress disorder, depression, and anxiety.

Despite the widespread nature of sexual exploitation during World War II, many women found ways to resist and fight back against their oppressors. Some women were able to escape from their captors, often with the help of resistance groups or sympathetic individuals.

Others engaged in acts of sabotage, working to undermine the war effort or disrupt the operations of the occupying forces.

One example of women's resistance to sexual exploitation was the story of the "Ravensbruck rabbits." These women were subjected to horrific medical experiments at the Ravensbruck concentration camp, including forced sterilization and other forms of physical torture. Despite the immense trauma they faced, the women worked together to support each other and maintain their dignity and humanity in the face of unspeakable cruelty.

THE AFTERMATH OF WAR

The aftermath of World War II saw a significant shift in the global political landscape, as countries around the world began the process of rebuilding and redefining their relationships with one another. The devastation wrought by the war had left many nations in ruins, and there was a sense of urgency to create a new world order that would prevent another catastrophic conflict from occurring. The post-World War II era was marked by the rise of two superpowers, the United States and the Soviet Union, and the tensions between these nations would come to define the international relations of the era. The period saw the emergence of new international organisations and the development of new diplomatic strategies, as nations sought to navigate the complex and often fraught landscape of global politics.

CHAPTER XXII: THE UNITED NATIONS

The creation of the United Nations (UN) is a remarkable story of international cooperation and diplomacy, born out of the devastating aftermath of World War II. As the world struggled to rebuild from the ruins of war and prevent another global conflict, the idea of a united and peaceful world began to take shape.

The origins of the UN can be traced back to the League of Nations, which was founded after World War I with the goal of promoting international cooperation and resolving conflicts through diplomacy. However, the League ultimately failed to prevent the outbreak of World War II, and a new approach was needed.

In 1941, as the war raged on, President Franklin D. Roosevelt of the United States and Prime Minister Winston Churchill of Great Britain met in Washington, D.C. to discuss the post-war world.

The meeting was held in secret, with only a small group of advisors present. Roosevelt and Churchill were keenly aware of the need for discretion, as the war was still raging, and their discussions could have far-reaching implications.

The two leaders discussed a wide range of issues, from military strategy to post-war reconstruction. But one topic in particular stood out: the idea of creating a new international organisation that could promote peace and security in the world.

Roosevelt and Churchill were both committed to the idea of international cooperation, and believed that a new organisation could help prevent future conflicts and promote a more stable world order. They envisioned an organisation that would bring together nations from around the world to work towards common goals and address global challenges.

The two leaders recognized that such an organisation would need to have a strong foundation in international law, and would require the support of the major powers in order to be effective.

They discussed the possibility of creating a body similar to the League of Nations, but with greater authority and a stronger commitment to collective security.

Despite their enthusiasm for the idea, Roosevelt and Churchill knew that creating a new international organisation would be a difficult and complex undertaking. They recognized that different nations would have different priorities and interests, and that achieving consensus would require careful negotiation and diplomacy.

Nevertheless, the two leaders were convinced that the creation of a new international organisation was essential for the future of the world. They believed that the lessons of the past had taught them the importance of international cooperation and the dangers of isolationism and unilateralism.

As the meeting came to a close, Roosevelt and Churchill agreed to continue working towards the creation of a new international organisation.

They knew that the road ahead would be long and difficult, but they were committed to the vision of a more peaceful and just world, and believed that a new international organisation could help make that vision a reality.

When representatives from 50 nations gathered in San Francisco for the United Nations Conference on International Organization in 1945, their vision became a reality. The conference was a historic meeting that brought together representatives from 50 nations to talk about the creation of a new global organisation that could advance world peace and security. Diplomats, politicians, and other leaders from all political parties were present, and they were all united in their desire to stop future wars and advance a more secure and equitable global order.

One of the key aspects of the conference was the focus on international law and the establishment of a system of collective security. The delegates recognized that the failure of the League of Nations to prevent the outbreak of the Second World War was due in large part to its lack of enforcement mechanisms and the unwillingness of some nations to abide by its decisions.

To address these shortcomings, the delegates worked to establish a new international organisation with stronger enforcement mechanisms and a greater commitment to collective security. They also sought to establish a system of international law that would be binding on all nations, and would provide a framework for resolving disputes and preventing conflicts.

Another key aspect of the conference was the focus on human rights and the establishment of a universal declaration of human rights. The delegates recognized that the atrocities committed during the war were a stark reminder of the need to protect the basic rights and freedoms of all people, and that a new international organisation could play a key role in promoting these values.

In addition to these key issues, the conference also addressed a range of other topics, from economic development to the establishment of a system for managing international disputes. The delegates worked tirelessly to negotiate and draft the text of the UN Charter, which would serve as the foundation for the new organisation.

Despite the challenges and disagreements, the delegates ultimately succeeded in reaching a consensus and establishing the United Nations. The UN Charter was signed on June 26, 1945, with representatives from all 50 countries present at the conference.

The role of the United Nations in the early years was multifaceted. One of its key functions was to promote international cooperation and dialogue, with the goal of preventing future conflicts. The UN provided a forum for countries to discuss and address global challenges, from economic development to human rights.

One of the UN's earliest and most important initiatives was the establishment of the International Court of Justice (ICJ), which was tasked with settling disputes between countries. The ICJ played a key role in resolving a number of high-profile disputes in the post-war period, including the Corfu Channel Case between Albania and the United Kingdom.

Another important role of the UN in this period was the establishment of the United Nations Relief and Rehabilitation Administration (UNRRA), which was tasked with providing humanitarian aid to those affected by the war. The UNRRA provided food, clothing, and medical supplies to millions of people, and helped to rebuild infrastructure and housing in devastated areas.

The UN also played a key role in the creation of the Universal Declaration of Human Rights, which was adopted by the General Assembly in 1948. The Declaration outlined a set of fundamental rights and freedoms that were to be protected by all nations, and provided a framework for promoting human dignity and equality around the world.

One of the biggest challenges faced by the UN in this period was the outbreak of the Korean War in 1950. The UN quickly mobilised to address the conflict, with the Security Council authorising the deployment of a multinational force to repel the North Korean invasion of South Korea.

While the conflict remained unresolved for years, the UN's intervention helped to prevent a wider war and demonstrated its commitment to maintaining peace and stability in the world.

Despite these successes, the UN faced a number of challenges in its early years. One of the biggest was the ongoing tensions between the United States and the Soviet Union, which had emerged as the world's two superpowers. The Cold War cast a shadow over the UN's work, with the two sides often unable to agree on key issues and initiatives.

Another challenge faced by the UN was the lack of resources and funding. The organisation relied heavily on contributions from member states, many of which were still struggling to rebuild in the aftermath of the war. This limited the UN's ability to carry out its mission effectively, and often led to delays and shortfalls in its programs and initiatives.

The creation of the United Nations was met with a wide range of reactions from citizens and nations around the world.

Some welcomed the UN as a beacon of hope in a world that had been ravaged by war, while others remained sceptical of its ability to address the complex challenges facing humanity.

Many citizens around the world were hopeful about the UN's potential to promote peace and prosperity. They saw the organisation as a way to bring countries together and prevent future conflicts. In the aftermath of World War II, there was a strong desire among many people for a more peaceful and just world order, and the UN seemed to offer a path towards that goal.

However, there were also many who remained sceptical of the UN's ability to live up to its promises. Some felt that the organisation was too weak and ineffective to address the complex challenges facing the world. Others were concerned about the balance of power within the UN, with some countries wielding more influence than others.

Nations around the world also had mixed reactions to the UN. Some saw it as a way to promote their interests and values on the global stage, while others were more cautious or even hostile towards the organisation.

The United States, for example, played a key role in the creation of the UN and remained a strong supporter of the organisation in its early years. However, as the Cold War intensified and tensions with the Soviet Union grew, some in the US government became more critical of the UN, seeing it as a forum that could be easily manipulated by their adversaries.

Other nations were more critical of the UN from the outset. The Soviet Union, for example, saw the organisation as a tool of the Western powers and was highly suspicious of its motives and actions. Other countries in the developing world were concerned about the unequal distribution of power within the UN, which they felt favoured the interests of the wealthy and powerful nations over the needs and concerns of smaller and less influential states.

Over the years, the reaction to the UN has continued to be mixed. While the organisation has had many successes in promoting peace, human rights, and development around the world, it has also faced criticism and scepticism from many quarters.

Some have argued that the UN is too bureaucratic and slow-moving to effectively address the complex challenges facing the world today. Others have criticised the organisation for being too beholden to the interests of its most powerful members, and for failing to live up to its own ideals in the face of political pressure and conflicting priorities.

CHAPTER XXIII: POST WAR GERMANY

The issue of rebuilding Germany was possibly the most complex one for the allies after WW2. With major cities and industrial centres reduced to rubble and a population that had been subject to intensive Nazi propaganda for over 10 years; how could Germany be formed into a modern Western Democracy?

The first steps towards rebuilding Germany were taken in the immediate aftermath of the war. The Allied powers, who had defeated Germany, imposed a series of strict conditions on the country, including the demilitarisation of its armed forces, the dismantling of its war industries, and the payment of massive reparations to the victorious nations.

ECONOMIC SANCTIONS

Germany was required to pay substantial reparations following World War II. The exact amount varied depending on the agreements and treaties signed by Germany and the Allied powers.

It is estimated that Germany paid around $31 billion in reparations in total, a sum that represented approximately 16% of the country's gross national product.

The major agreements that required Germany to pay reparations include the Potsdam Agreement of 1945, which set the total amount at $20 billion, and the London Agreement of 1953, which reduced the amount to $7 billion. The remaining $4 billion was paid through bilateral agreements between Germany and individual Allied powers.

It's worth noting that the burden of these reparations fell heavily on the German people, and contributed to a period of economic hardship in post-war Germany. The issue of reparations remains a contentious one to this day.

The reparations were primarily intended to compensate the Allies for the damage caused by the war. This included compensation for physical damage to buildings and infrastructure, as well as compensation for loss of life and injury suffered by Allied soldiers and civilians.

The reparations were also intended to help rebuild the economies of the countries that had been devastated by the war. This was especially important for countries like France and Great Britain, which had suffered significant damage to their economies and infrastructure during the war.

To pay the reparations, Germany was required to surrender a significant amount of its industrial and agricultural production to the Allies. This included coal, steel, and other raw materials, as well as machinery and other equipment. The production of these goods was vital to the rebuilding of the German economy, and their loss had a significant impact on the country's ability to recover from the war.

The amount of industrial and agricultural production that Germany was required to surrender to the Allies was staggering. The country was forced to give up a significant portion of its coal production, which was vital for the operation of its factories and power plants. This had a significant impact on the country's ability to rebuild its infrastructure and modernise its economy.

Germany was also required to surrender a significant portion of its steel production to the Allies. This was a vital resource for the rebuilding of the country's infrastructure, including roads, bridges, and buildings. The loss of this resource made it much more difficult for Germany to rebuild its economy and infrastructure in the post-war period.

In addition to coal and steel, Germany was also required to surrender a significant amount of other raw materials, such as copper, aluminium, and zinc. These materials were vital for the production of machinery and other equipment, and their loss had a significant impact on the country's ability to modernise and rebuild its economy.

The loss of agricultural production was also a significant blow to Germany's economy. The country was required to surrender a significant amount of its agricultural production to the Allies, including wheat, barley, and oats. This had a significant impact on the country's ability to feed its population, and contributed to a period of food shortages and economic hardship.

In addition to the economic impact, the payment of reparations also had a profound psychological impact on the German people. For many Germans, the idea of paying reparations was seen as a sign of weakness and humiliation. They felt that their country had been unfairly targeted by the Allies and that the reparations were a form of punishment that was intended to cripple the German economy and humiliate its people.

Many Germans also felt a deep sense of shame in the aftermath of the war. They were forced to confront the atrocities that had been committed by their country during the war, including the Holocaust and other crimes against humanity. This led to a sense of guilt and shame that was difficult for many Germans to shake off, even years after the end of the war.

The reparations also had a significant impact on the German economy and society. The loss of industrial and agricultural production, as well as the massive financial burden of paying reparations, made it difficult for Germany to rebuild and recover in the aftermath of the war.

This led to a period of economic hardship and instability, which contributed to a sense of despair and hopelessness among many Germans.

The psychological impact of the reparations was also felt on a personal level by many Germans. Families were torn apart by the war, with many losing loved ones in the conflict. Those who survived the war were left to deal with the emotional scars of the conflict, including PTSD and other psychological trauma.

Despite the challenges, however, many Germans were able to rebuild their lives and their country in the aftermath of the war. They worked hard to overcome the psychological impact of the reparations and to build a better future for themselves and their families. Through their resilience and determination, they were able to turn the tide and emerge as a strong and prosperous nation in the post-war period.

A NATION DIVIDED

After the War, Germany was divided territorially among the victorious Allied powers: the United States, the Soviet Union, Great Britain, and France.

The division of Germany was a result of the Potsdam Conference held in July and August of 1945, where the Allied leaders decided on the fate of Germany and its territories.

As a result of the conference, Germany was divided into four occupation zones, with each Allied power administering one zone. The Soviet Union took control of the eastern part of Germany, which included the capital city of Berlin. The United States, Great Britain, and France administered the western part of Germany.

The division of Germany was not just territorial, but also political and ideological. The Soviet Union saw an opportunity to spread communism into Germany and establish a socialist state in the eastern part of the country. Under Stalin's leadership, the Soviet Union implemented policies and tactics to establish a communist regime in East Germany.

Stalin's first step was to establish a puppet government in East Germany, known as the German Democratic Republic (GDR).

The GDR was established in October 1949 and was led by Walter Ulbricht, a communist and loyal follower of Stalin.

The new government immediately set out to implement communist policies, nationalising industries and redistributing land. The GDR also established a planned economy, with the government controlling production and distribution.

In addition to these economic policies, the GDR also implemented strict censorship and control of the media. All media outlets were controlled by the government, and any criticism of the government was strictly forbidden. The government also established a secret police force, known as the Stasi, to monitor and suppress any opposition to the communist regime.

The GDR also implemented policies to promote socialist education and culture, with a focus on Marxism-Leninism. Schools were required to teach socialist principles, and the arts were subject to strict censorship and control.

The establishment of the communist regime in East Germany led to a mass exodus of East Germans to the West, as they sought to escape the oppressive regime. In response, the GDR implemented strict border controls, which eventually led to the construction of the Berlin Wall in 1961, separating East and West Berlin.

Under Stalin's leadership, the Soviet Union also established a system of satellite states throughout Eastern Europe, with communist governments loyal to Moscow. These satellite states were used to spread Soviet influence and to counter the influence of Western powers in Europe.

The communist regime in East Germany was marked by economic stagnation and political oppression. The planned economy failed to produce the goods and services needed by the people, leading to shortages and long waiting lists for basic necessities. The strict censorship and control of the media stifled dissent and opposition, leading to a culture of fear and suspicion.

The western powers, however, saw an opportunity to establish democracy in Germany and worked to establish a democratic government in the western part of the country.

The first step in establishing democracy in West Germany was to create a new constitution. The Basic Law for the Federal Republic of Germany was adopted in May 1949 and established the principles of democracy, freedom, and the rule of law. The constitution also established a federal system of government, with power shared between the central government and the states.

The new government in West Germany was led by Chancellor Konrad Adenauer, a Christian Democrat who was committed to establishing a democratic and prosperous Germany. Adenauer worked closely with the western powers to rebuild the German economy and establish democratic institutions.

One of the key priorities for the new government was to rebuild the German economy.

The western powers provided significant financial assistance to help rebuild the country, and the German government implemented policies to promote economic growth and stability. These policies included the privatisation of industries, the promotion of international trade, and the establishment of a social welfare system.

The government also worked to establish democratic institutions, such as free and fair elections and an independent judiciary. The press and media were also free to report on government activities and hold officials accountable for their actions.

In addition to these political and economic reforms, the government in West Germany also worked to promote human rights and social justice. The country became a leader in the promotion of gender equality and social welfare programs, such as healthcare and education.

The establishment of democracy in West Germany was not without its challenges, however. The country was still grappling with the legacy of the Nazi regime and the devastation of the war.

There were also tensions between East and West Germany, as the Soviet Union sought to spread communism throughout Europe.

Despite these challenges, the government in West Germany remained committed to democracy and worked to establish strong relationships with its Western allies. The country became a key member of the European Union and NATO, working closely with its partners to promote peace and stability in Europe.

Moreover, the city of Berlin itself was also split into four occupation zones administered by the same powers. It is important to note that Berlin sits in the Northeast of Germany, deep into Soviet controlled East Germany.

Initially, the four powers worked together to administer the city, but tensions between the Soviet Union and the Western powers soon emerged. In June 1948, the Soviet Union blockaded West Berlin, cutting off all rail, road, and water access to the city in an attempt to force the Western powers out.

The Western powers responded by launching the Berlin Airlift. The airlift involved a massive logistical effort to transport supplies, food, and fuel to the people of West Berlin, who were cut off from the rest of the world by the Soviet blockade.

The airlift was an extraordinary feat of engineering, as planes flew around the clock, delivering supplies to West Berlin every few minutes. At its peak, the airlift involved over 1,000 flights per day, with planes landing and taking off every 90 seconds.

The airlift was not without its risks. Pilots had to navigate through Soviet airspace, and there were concerns that the Soviet Union might attempt to shoot down the planes. However, the pilots and ground crew worked tirelessly to ensure that the supplies were delivered safely to the people of West Berlin.

The airlift was also an enormous financial and logistical challenge. The Western powers had to mobilise their resources to support the airlift, and they had to overcome significant logistical challenges to transport the supplies to Berlin.

Despite these challenges, the airlift was a success. The people of West Berlin were able to receive the supplies they needed to survive, and the Soviet Union eventually lifted the blockade in May 1949.

The Berlin Airlift was a defining moment in the early years of the Cold War. It showed the resolve of the Western powers to stand up to Soviet aggression, and it demonstrated the power of international cooperation in the face of adversity.

The airlift also had a profound impact on the people of Berlin. The people of West Berlin were grateful for the support they received from the Western powers, and the airlift became a symbol of hope and resilience in the face of adversity.

Despite the tensions, the four powers continued to administer their respective sectors of the city, with the Soviet Union controlling the eastern part of the city and the Western powers controlling the western part of the city. The border between the two parts of the city was marked by checkpoints, and travel was tightly controlled.

The division of the city had a profound impact on the lives of the people who lived there. Families and friends were separated by the border, and many people lost their homes and businesses as a result of the division.

In the Soviet-controlled East Berlin, the government sought to establish a communist state. The government took control of industries and agriculture, and political dissent was suppressed. Many people fled to West Berlin in search of greater freedom and opportunities.

In contrast, West Berlin became a symbol of democracy and freedom. The government in West Berlin worked closely with the Western powers to rebuild the city and establish democratic institutions. The city became a beacon of hope for those living under communist rule in Eastern Europe.

Despite the division of the city, there were still connections between the two parts of the city. Families and friends remained in contact, and there were some trade and cultural exchanges between the two parts of the city.

However, tensions between the two parts of the city remained high, and there were frequent incidents of violence and protests. In 1961, the government in East Berlin erected the Berlin Wall, which divided the city into two parts and marked the border between the two parts of the city.

The construction of the wall further divided the city and had a profound impact on the lives of the people who lived there. Families and friends were separated, and many people lost their homes and businesses as a result of the division.

DENAZIFICATION

In order to rebuild Germany, it was essential to address the root cause of its downfall - the ideology of Nazism and the individuals who had supported it. The process of denazification was initiated by the Allied powers with the aim of purging Nazi influence from German society and establishing a democratic and free Germany.

Denazification was a complex and challenging process, involving the identification and prosecution of Nazi war criminals, the removal of Nazi influence from the government and other institutions, and the re-education of the German population.

The Allied Control Council (ACC) was tasked with the difficult mission of rebuilding Germany and eradicating the Nazi ideology from its society. The process of denazification involved the removal of Nazi symbols, the arrest and prosecution of Nazi leaders, and the re-education of the German population to prevent the resurgence of Nazi ideas.

The ACC played a critical role in this process, as it was responsible for enacting laws and policies that would achieve these goals. One of the first steps taken by the ACC was the issuance of the Control Council Law No. 1, which prohibited Nazi activities and organisations in Germany. This law also mandated the removal of Nazi symbols and the confiscation of property belonging to former Nazis.

The ACC also established tribunals to prosecute war criminals and those responsible for atrocities committed during the war. These trials were held in Nuremberg, with the first trial beginning in November 1945. The Nuremberg Trials were the first international war crimes tribunals and established the principle that individuals could be held accountable for crimes against humanity.

In addition to these legal measures, the Allies also sought to re-educate the German population about the dangers of Nazi ideology and to promote democratic values and human rights. This was done through the establishment of schools and universities that emphasised the importance of individual freedoms, civil liberties, and the rule of law. These institutions also taught the principles of a market economy and stressed the need for social welfare programs.

The implementation of denazification was not without its challenges as many Germans still believed in the ideals of the Nazi party and were resistant to change.

There were also concerns about the effectiveness of the denazification process, particularly in terms of removing former Nazis from positions of power in government, industry, and academia.

One of the key sources of resistance to denazification was the fact that many former Nazis were able to hide their past affiliations and continue to hold positions of influence in post-war Germany. This was particularly true in the field of education, where many former Nazi teachers and administrators were able to continue their work without facing any repercussions.

Another source of resistance to denazification was the fact that many Germans saw the process as an attack on their national identity. They felt that denazification was being imposed upon them by foreign powers and resented the fact that they were not allowed to determine their own future.

In addition, there were also practical challenges to implementing denazification. Many former Nazis were able to avoid detection or punishment by fleeing to other countries, such as Argentina or Egypt.

Others were able to hide their past affiliations or were able to secure false identities that allowed them to avoid detection.

Despite these challenges, the Allies persisted in their efforts to implement denazification. They established tribunals and courts to prosecute war criminals and other individuals responsible for atrocities committed during the war. They also implemented laws and directives that banned Nazi activities and symbols and sought to promote democratic values and human rights.

Over time, these efforts began to bear fruit. Many former Nazis were removed from positions of power, and the influence of the Nazi party waned. The re-education of the German population also played a critical role in creating a new, democratic Germany that was firmly committed to human rights and the rule of law.

CHAPTER XXIV: POST WAR JAPAN

1945 saw Japan left in ruins. Its cities lay in shambles, and its people were starving. The country's once-mighty military had been defeated, and its economy was in tatters. In the midst of all this destruction, the Japanese people were left to pick up the pieces and rebuild their country from scratch.

Emperor Hirohito stood before the nation, his voice crackling over the radio. For the first time in Japanese history, he spoke directly to his subjects, announcing Japan's surrender to the Allied powers. The news was met with disbelief, anger, and despair. The nation had been taught that surrender was worse than death, and now they were being asked to do just that.

DIVIDED TERRITORY

The aftermath of World War II saw Japan divided into two spheres of influence, with the United States and the Soviet Union each occupying a portion of the country.

This division had profound implications for Japan's post-war reconstruction and its subsequent development as a nation.

The occupation of Japan began on August 28th, 1945, when General Douglas MacArthur arrived in Tokyo. MacArthur was appointed Supreme Commander of the Allied Powers (SCAP) and given broad authority to govern Japan. His mission was to demilitarise Japan, reform its political and economic systems, and oversee its reconstruction.

The first order of business was to draft a new constitution. The SCAP brought in a team of experts, including Japanese legal scholars and American advisors, to write a new charter for Japan. The resulting document, known as the Constitution of Japan, was ratified in 1947 and has remained the foundation of Japanese governance ever since.

The constitution established a parliamentary system of government, with a bicameral legislature, a bill of rights, and a strong executive branch.

It also renounced war as an instrument of national policy and declared that Japan would forever renounce its right to maintain military forces. These provisions were intended to ensure that Japan would never again become a militaristic nation and would instead focus on economic development and peaceful cooperation with other nations.

To support Japan's reconstruction, the SCAP provided aid and technical assistance, and it encouraged the development of private enterprise. The result was a rapid transformation of the Japanese economy. Within a few years, Japan had emerged as a major industrial power, with a thriving export sector and a high standard of living.

The SCAP also implemented a series of social and cultural reforms. Women were given the right to vote, and their role in society was revaluated. The strict social hierarchy that had defined Japanese society for centuries was challenged, and new forms of expression, such as rock music and fashion, were embraced by young people.

At the same time, the Japanese government was encouraged to acknowledge and apologise for its past actions, including its role in the war and its treatment of its Asian neighbours.

The occupation of Japan lasted from 1945 to 1952, during which time the country underwent a remarkable transformation. Japan emerged from the war not as a defeated nation, but as a vibrant democracy and an economic powerhouse. The legacy of the occupation can still be seen in Japan today, from its democratic institutions to its robust economy.

However, the occupation was not without its controversies. Many Japanese resented the presence of foreign troops on their soil and chafed under the restrictions imposed by the SCAP. There were also tensions between the United States and Japan over issues such as the status of the emperor and the role of the military in post-war Japan.

The Soviet Union saw Japan as an opportunity to expand its sphere of influence in the region and to create a socialist state.

Unlike the United States, which was focused on rebuilding Japan's economy and creating a democratic government, the Soviet Union was more interested in extracting resources and imposing its political system on the Japanese people.

Under Soviet occupation, the northern part of Japan was subjected to a series of reforms aimed at transforming the region into a communist stronghold. These reforms included the confiscation of land from large landowners, the redistribution of land to peasants, and the nationalisation of key industries.

The Soviet Union also established a communist government in the north, with the aim of creating a socialist state. The new government was led by the Japanese Communist Party and was heavily influenced by Soviet advisors. The Soviet Union hoped that the establishment of a communist government in northern Japan would serve as a model for other countries in the region and help spread communism throughout Asia.

However, the Soviet Union's occupation of northern Japan had little lasting impact on the country's political or economic development. The policies implemented by the Soviet Union did little to contribute to the country's long-term growth and prosperity. The Soviet Union's focus on extracting resources and imposing its political system on the Japanese people did not lead to the creation of a sustainable economy or a stable political system.

In addition, the Soviet Union's occupation of northern Japan was characterised by repression and brutality. The Soviet Union's policies led to the suppression of political dissent and the imprisonment and execution of those who opposed the new regime. The people of northern Japan were subjected to a harsh regime of censorship and propaganda, and many were forced to participate in Soviet-style mass rallies and parades.

Despite these efforts, the Soviet Union's occupation of northern Japan was relatively short-lived. The Soviet Union withdrew its troops from Japan in the early 1950s, and Japan became an independent nation once again.

The legacy of the Soviet Union's occupation of northern Japan can still be seen in the region today, however. The northern part of Japan has a different political and economic landscape from the rest of the country, and the legacy of Soviet-style communism is still evident in the region's political culture.

THE ECONOMIC MIRACLE

The Japanese Economic Miracle began in the 1950s and lasted until the early 1990s. During this time, Japan's economy experienced rapid growth and modernization, transforming the country into one of the world's leading economic powers. The Japanese Economic Miracle was fuelled by a combination of government policies, private enterprise, and a strong work ethic among the Japanese people.

The policies implemented by the Japanese government during this time played a crucial role in fuelling the country's economic success.

The first key policy implemented for the Japanese Economic Miracle was the government's investment in infrastructure and industry.

The government established a series of policies aimed at promoting economic growth, including investing in transportation, telecommunications, and energy infrastructure. This investment laid the foundation for Japan's economic success, creating a modern, efficient economy that was able to compete on the global stage. The government also established industrial parks and provided subsidies and tax incentives to attract foreign investment, which helped to further stimulate economic growth.

The second key policy was the government's focus on promoting exports. The Japanese government recognized the importance of exporting goods to fuel economic growth, and as a result, established policies that encouraged companies to focus on exports. This included providing subsidies for exporting companies, reducing trade barriers, and promoting international trade fairs. The government's focus on exports helped to create a strong demand for Japanese products in foreign markets, which further fuelled the country's economic growth.

Another important policy implemented for the Japanese Economic Miracle was the government's support for research and development. The government recognized the importance of innovation in driving economic growth and established policies to encourage companies to invest in research and development. This included providing tax incentives for R&D spending, establishing research institutes, and providing funding for universities and research institutions. This support for R&D helped to create a culture of innovation in Japan, leading to the development of ground breaking technologies and products.

The fourth policy implemented for the Japanese Economic Miracle was the government's commitment to education and training. The Japanese government recognized that a skilled workforce was essential for economic growth and established policies to promote education and training. This included expanding access to education, investing in vocational training programs, and encouraging lifelong learning. This commitment to education and training helped to create a highly skilled workforce in Japan, which was essential for the country's economic success.

Lastly, the government established policies to encourage cooperation between the public and private sectors. The government recognized that cooperation between the two sectors was essential for economic growth and established policies to encourage collaboration. This included establishing industry associations, providing funding for joint research projects, and promoting public-private partnerships. This cooperation between the public and private sectors helped to stimulate innovation and create new opportunities for economic growth.

The Japanese Economic Miracle was also fuelled by the strong work ethic of the Japanese people. Japanese workers were known for their dedication and commitment to their jobs, working long hours and often sacrificing their personal lives for the sake of their companies. This dedication helped to create a culture of innovation and competitiveness in the Japanese workplace, which further fuelled the country's economic success.

As a result of these factors, Japan's economy grew at an unprecedented rate.

From the 1950s to the 1970s, Japan's economy grew at an average annual rate of more than 10%, far outpacing the growth rates of other industrialised countries. By the 1980s, Japan had become one of the world's largest economies, and its corporations had become household names, with brands like Sony, Toyota, and Honda becoming synonymous with quality and innovation.

However, the Japanese Economic Miracle came to an end in the early 1990s, as a result of a series of factors, including an asset bubble, an ageing population, and increased competition from other countries. Despite this, the legacy of the Japanese Economic Miracle still lives on today. Japan's economy remains one of the largest and most successful in the world, and the country is still known for its innovative technology, high-quality products, and strong work ethic.

A CULTURAL SHIFT

The end of World War II brought about significant changes to Japanese society, including cultural changes that continue to shape the country today.

One of the most notable cultural changes after World War II was the shift in values and beliefs. Prior to the war, Japan had a strong sense of national pride and loyalty, which was reflected in its cultural values. However, the defeat in the war led to a revaluation of these values, as many Japanese citizens began to question the country's militaristic past. This led to a shift in values towards a more pacifist and democratic mindset, with a greater emphasis on individual rights and freedoms.

Another cultural change in Japan after World War II was the influence of American culture. During the Allied occupation of Japan, American troops brought with them their own culture, including music, fashion, and cinema. This had a significant impact on Japanese culture, as young people began to adopt American styles and attitudes. This led to the emergence of a new youth culture in Japan, which was characterised by a focus on individualism, consumerism, and self-expression.

The post-war period also saw a rise in women's rights and gender equality.

Prior to the war, women in Japan were expected to fulfil traditional roles as wives and mothers, with limited opportunities for education and employment. However, the war had led to a shortage of male workers, which meant that women were given new opportunities to work outside the home. This led to a push for women's rights and greater gender equality, with more women entering the workforce and pursuing higher education.

Another cultural change in Japan after World War II was the growth of popular culture. As Japan's economy began to recover, the country saw the emergence of new forms of entertainment, such as manga, anime, and video games. These forms of popular culture quickly became a part of everyday life for many Japanese citizens, and had a significant impact on the country's cultural identity. They also became a major export for Japan, with anime and manga becoming popular around the world.

Finally, the post-war period also saw a revival of traditional Japanese culture. With the country's defeat in the war, many Japanese citizens began to look back to their cultural roots, and there was a renewed interest in traditional Japanese arts and crafts.

This led to a revival of traditional forms of art, such as calligraphy, flower arranging, and tea ceremonies, which had been neglected during the war years.

JAPAN'S PLACE IN THE WORLD

In the decades that followed the end of the War, Japan's influence on international trade and finance grew rapidly, and Japanese companies began to acquire major firms around the world. In addition to economic power, Japan also became a major cultural influence, exporting everything from anime and manga to fashion and food.

One of the most significant ways in which Japan exerted its influence on the global stage was through technological innovation. The country was at the forefront of advances in electronics and robotics, and Japanese firms such as Sony and Panasonic became household names around the world. Japan's technological prowess was also on display in the transportation sector, with companies such as Honda, Toyota, and Nissan becoming global leaders in the production of automobiles.

Japan's influence on the global stage was not without controversy, however. As the country's economic power grew, so too did concerns about its impact on the global economy. Japan's trade surplus with the United States and other countries led to accusations of unfair trade practices and protectionism, and tensions between Japan and other nations were often high.

In addition to economic and technological influence, Japan also became a significant player in international diplomacy. The country has been an active participant in the United Nations and other international organisations, and has been a vocal advocate for peace and disarmament.

One of the earliest examples of Japan's involvement in international diplomacy was its participation in the San Francisco Peace Treaty of 1951. This treaty officially ended World War II for Japan and helped to establish the country as a peaceful member of the international community. Through this treaty, Japan renounced war as a sovereign right and pledged to promote international cooperation and the peaceful settlement of disputes.

The treaty also helped to set the stage for Japan's involvement in international organisations such as the United Nations.

Japan's membership in the United Nations was a significant step in its post-war diplomacy efforts. The country joined the organisation in 1956 and has since played an active role in promoting peace and security around the world. Japan has been a strong supporter of the UN's efforts to promote disarmament and non-proliferation, and has been a leading contributor to UN peacekeeping missions. In addition, Japan has also been a vocal advocate for human rights and has supported efforts to promote sustainable development and combat climate change.

One of the most significant ways in which Japan has exerted its influence in international diplomacy is through its alliance with the United States. The two countries established a security alliance in 1951, which has been a cornerstone of Japan's foreign policy ever since.

The alliance has been instrumental in maintaining peace and stability in the Asia-Pacific region, and Japan has provided significant military support to the United States in conflicts around the world. At the same time, Japan has also pursued its own diplomatic efforts, engaging with neighbouring countries and playing an active role in regional organisations such as the Association of Southeast Asian Nations (ASEAN).

Despite its efforts in international diplomacy, Japan has also faced challenges and criticisms from other countries. One of the most significant issues has been its historical legacy, particularly in relation to its actions during World War II. Japan's handling of issues such as the use of "comfort women" during the war has drawn criticism from other countries, particularly South Korea and China. At the same time, Japan's territorial disputes with neighbouring countries, particularly over the Senkaku/Diaoyu Islands, have also created tensions in the region.

CHAPTER XXV: POST WAR ITALY

Italy emerged from the war heavily damaged both economically and socially, having suffered significant losses in both human lives and material resources. However, despite these challenges, the post-war period in Italy was characterised by a significant transformation in the country's social, political, and economic landscape.

THE POLITICAL LANDSCAPE

In the aftermath of World War II, Italy found itself in a state of political turmoil. The fascist government of Benito Mussolini had been overthrown, and the country was occupied by Allied forces until 1946. In the years that followed, Italy's political landscape underwent a significant transformation, as the country struggled to establish a stable and democratic system of government.

The first post-war elections were held in 1946, and the country's new constitution was approved in 1947.

The constitution established a parliamentary system of government, with a bicameral legislature consisting of a Chamber of Deputies and a Senate. The president of the republic was elected by an electoral college composed of members of parliament and regional representatives, and the prime minister was appointed by the president.

One of the major sources of tension was the issue of land reform. The Italian Communist Party had campaigned on a platform of land reform, advocating for the redistribution of land from wealthy landowners to poor farmers. The Christian Democratic Party was initially supportive of the idea, but as the government began to implement reforms, tensions between the two parties began to rise.

The issue came to a head in May 1947, when the Communist Party staged a series of strikes and protests in northern Italy. The protests were met with a heavy-handed response from the government, and clashes between protesters and police led to several deaths. The government responded by banning the Communist Party, which led to a wave of protests and strikes throughout the country.

The ban on the Communist Party was not the only source of political instability during this period. There were also significant conflicts within the Christian Democratic Party, as various factions jockeyed for power and influence. The party was led by Alcide De Gasperi, who sought to maintain a delicate balance between left-wing and right-wing factions. However, his attempts to do so were frequently thwarted by infighting within the party.

The period of instability came to a head in June 1948, when Italy held a crucial national election. The election was seen as a referendum on the country's political direction, and the Christian Democratic Party faced stiff competition from a range of left-wing and right-wing parties. In the end, the Christian Democrats emerged victorious, winning a significant majority of the vote and securing a mandate to continue their policy of centrist politics. The election marked a turning point in Italian politics, as the Christian Democratic Party went on to dominate Italian politics for the next four decades.

Under the leadership of Alcide De Gasperi, the Christian Democratic Party pursued a policy of centrist politics, seeking to maintain a delicate balance between left-wing and right-wing factions. The party's success in doing so was largely due to its ability to build alliances with other parties, including the Socialists and the Communists, who were willing to support the government in exchange for concessions on key policy issues.

However, the period of political stability that followed was not without its challenges. The country experienced periodic political crises, including a major crisis in 1964, when the government of Prime Minister Aldo Moro collapsed following a dispute over labour laws. The country also experienced a wave of political violence in the late 1960s and early 1970s, as leftist and right-wing groups clashed in the streets.

Despite these challenges, Italy emerged from the post-war period as a modern and democratic country. The country's membership in the European Union, which it helped to found in 1957, cemented its place as a key player in European politics and economics.

Today, Italy is known for its vibrant and dynamic political landscape, which is characterised by a wide range of political parties and interest groups.

ECONOMIC RECOVERY

In the aftermath of World War II, Italy was faced with the daunting task of rebuilding its economy and infrastructure. The war had left the country in ruins, with factories and farms destroyed, transportation networks in disarray, and millions of people displaced. However, despite the challenges, Italy was able to embark on a remarkable period of economic recovery and development.

The key to Italy's economic recovery was the Marshall Plan, a program of economic aid provided by the United States and other Western nations.

One of the most important aspects of the Marshall Plan was its support for Italy's industrial sector. The country had long been known for its manufacturing prowess, but the war had left many factories in ruins.

With the help of Marshall Plan funds, Italy was able to rebuild its industrial base, modernise its factories, and expand its production capacity. This allowed Italian businesses to compete on the international stage and export goods to markets around the world.

In addition to supporting industry, the Marshall Plan also provided assistance for infrastructure projects. The funds were used to repair and expand transportation networks, build new roads and bridges, and improve ports and airports. This helped to facilitate trade and commerce, and made it easier for Italian businesses to connect with international markets.

The Marshall Plan also provided support for the agricultural sector. Italy had long been an agricultural powerhouse, but the war had destroyed many farms and disrupted food production. Marshall Plan funds were used to provide technical assistance to farmers, improve irrigation systems, and expand research and development programs. This allowed Italian agriculture to recover and expand, and helped to ensure that the country had a secure food supply.

Perhaps most importantly, the Marshall Plan helped to stabilise the Italian economy and promote political stability. The war had left the country in chaos, with high levels of inflation, unemployment, and social unrest. Marshall Plan funds were used to stabilise the economy, reduce inflation, and create jobs. This helped to reduce social and political tensions, and contributed to the growth of Italy's democratic institutions.

The impact of the Marshall Plan on Italy was immense. The aid package provided crucial support that allowed Italy to rebuild its economy and infrastructure, and establish itself as a major player on the international stage. The country's industrial sector expanded rapidly, allowing Italian businesses to compete on the global market. The infrastructure improvements facilitated trade and commerce, and helped to connect Italy with the rest of the world. The agricultural sector was able to recover and expand, ensuring that the country had a secure food supply. And perhaps most importantly, the Marshall Plan helped to stabilise the economy and promote political stability, contributing to the growth of Italy's democratic institutions.

The growth of the manufacturing sector was also supported by improvements in transportation infrastructure. The Italian government invested heavily in building new highways and railways, making it easier for goods to be transported around the country and to international markets.

Another important factor in Italy's economic recovery was the growth of tourism. Italy's rich cultural heritage, beautiful scenery, and sunny climate made it a popular destination for tourists from around the world. The tourism industry provided employment for millions of people and generated significant revenue for the country.

The economic recovery and development of Italy had a profound impact on the country's social and political landscape. The growth of the economy created new opportunities for people, providing employment and increasing standards of living. The country's newfound prosperity also helped to strengthen democratic institutions and support the growth of civil society.

However, the process of economic recovery and development was not without its challenges.

The growth of the manufacturing sector led to significant environmental problems, as factories and industrial facilities polluted the air and water. The rapid pace of development also led to urbanisation, as people moved from rural areas to cities in search of employment. This created new social and economic problems, including overcrowding and a lack of affordable housing.

SOCIAL CHANGES

Italy's post-World War II economic recovery was accompanied by significant social changes and challenges. One of the most important of these was the emergence of regional differences and identities, which had significant implications for Italy's social and political landscape.

Italy had always been a regionally diverse country, with distinct cultures, dialects, and traditions. However, the post-war period saw the emergence of these regional identities as a political force. Many regions began to demand greater autonomy and political power, challenging the centralised authority of the Italian state.

One of the most prominent examples of this was the movement for autonomy in the northern regions of Italy, particularly Lombardy and Veneto. These regions were some of the wealthiest in the country, and their inhabitants began to question the fairness of the central government's distribution of resources. They argued that they were being unfairly taxed and that their contributions to the national economy were not being adequately recognized.

The movement for autonomy in the north was met with resistance from the Italian government, which feared that it could lead to the fragmentation of the country. However, the movement gained momentum in the 1980s and 1990s, culminating in the passage of a law in 2001 that granted greater autonomy to several northern regions.

The regional differences and identities also had implications for Italy's social and cultural landscape. For example, the northern regions tended to be more industrialised and secular, while the southern regions were more agricultural and religious.

These differences contributed to the development of distinct cultural identities and traditions, which were celebrated and valued by the inhabitants of each region.

However, the regional differences and identities also posed challenges for Italy's social cohesion. The country had historically been characterised by a strong sense of national identity, but the emergence of regional identities challenged this idea. Some argued that the emphasis on regional identities could lead to the fragmentation of the country and undermine its ability to address common challenges and problems.

In addition to the regional differences, Italy also faced significant social challenges in the post-war period. These included issues related to immigration, gender equality, and social justice.

Immigration was a major issue in Italy, as the country experienced significant inflows of migrants from other parts of Europe and from former Italian colonies in Africa. The influx of immigrants led to tensions between different ethnic and cultural groups, as well as challenges related to integration and social cohesion.

Gender equality was another issue that Italy faced in the post-war period. The country had a conservative social and cultural landscape, which was reflected in its laws and policies. Women faced significant barriers to equal participation in the workforce and politics, and domestic violence and sexual harassment were significant problems.

Finally, social justice was a key challenge for Italy in the post-war period. The country had a highly unequal distribution of wealth and income, with many people living in poverty and facing significant barriers to social mobility. This led to social tensions and political instability, as people became increasingly frustrated with the lack of opportunities and the failure of the government to address these issues.

ITALY'S PLACE IN THE WORLD

Italy played a significant role in the post-World War II world, both in terms of its position in the global community and its domestic policies.

After the war, Italy was devastated, with its economy in ruins and its infrastructure badly damaged.

The country faced significant challenges in rebuilding its economy and society, but it also had an opportunity to redefine its place in the world.

One of the most significant steps Italy took in the post-war period was to align itself with the United States and the Western powers. Italy had traditionally been aligned with Germany and the Axis powers during World War II, but it quickly shifted its allegiance to the United States after the war.

The decision to align with the Western powers was not an easy one for Italy, with many Italians seeing them as imperialist and hostile to Italian interests. However, the realities of the post-war world made it clear that Italy could not go it alone. The country needed economic assistance and political support if it was going to rebuild and emerge as a major power in the post-war world.

One of the key factors that drove Italy's alignment with the Western powers was the threat posed by the Soviet Union and its allies.

The Soviet Union had emerged from the war as a major world power, and it was actively seeking to expand its influence in Europe and around the world.

Italy's leaders recognized that they could not stand up to the Soviet threat on their own. They needed the support of the United States and its Western allies if they were going to resist Soviet expansionism and maintain their independence.

This alignment had significant implications for Italy's foreign policy, as the country became an important member of the Western alliance against the Soviet Union and its allies. Italy was a founding member of the North Atlantic Treaty Organization (NATO), and it played an active role in the alliance, hosting U.S. military bases and contributing troops to NATO missions around the world.

Italy's alignment with the Western powers also had important cultural and social implications. The country became a centre of Western culture, with its fashion, art, and cuisine becoming globally recognized symbols of Italian excellence.

CHAPTER XXVI: THE POST WAR ALLIES

SOVIET UNION

The end of World War II saw the Soviet Union emerge as a victorious superpower. However, the post-World War II situation for the Soviet Union was complex and challenging, as it faced a range of economic, political, and social issues that needed to be addressed.

One of the most pressing issues that the Soviet Union faced was the need to rebuild its economy in the aftermath of the war. The Soviet Union had suffered extensive damage and destruction as a result of the war, and its infrastructure had been severely weakened.

The rebuilding effort began with a focus on agriculture. The Soviet government recognized that in order to rebuild the country's economy, it needed to first ensure that its people had enough to eat.

The government implemented a series of agricultural reforms, including the collectivization of farms and the introduction of new farming techniques. These reforms were successful, and the country was able to produce enough food to meet the needs of its citizens.

With its agricultural sector stabilised, the Soviet Union turned its attention to its industrial sector. The country had been a major industrial power before the war, and it was determined to regain its status as a leading industrial nation. The government implemented a series of industrial reforms, including the nationalisation of industry and the introduction of new technologies. These reforms were successful, and the country was able to rebuild its industrial base and regain its status as a leading industrial power.

One of the key factors in the Soviet Union's successful rebuilding effort was its commitment to education and scientific research. The government recognized that in order to rebuild its economy and infrastructure, it needed to have a highly educated and skilled workforce.

It invested heavily in education, and encouraged its citizens to pursue advanced degrees and engage in scientific research. This focus on education and research led to a number of technological breakthroughs, which helped to drive the country's economic growth.

Despite these successes, however, the Soviet Union continued to face a number of challenges in its rebuilding effort. One of the biggest challenges was a shortage of resources. The country had been devastated by the war, and it was difficult to obtain the resources it needed to rebuild. In order to address this issue, the government implemented a series of reforms aimed at increasing the efficiency of resource usage. These reforms were successful, and the country was able to make the most of the limited resources available to it.

Another challenge the Soviet Union faced was a shortage of skilled labour. Many of the country's skilled workers had been killed during the war, and it was difficult to find enough skilled workers to rebuild the country's infrastructure. In order to address this issue, the government implemented a series of training programs aimed at developing a new generation of skilled workers.

These programs were successful, and the country was able to rebuild its infrastructure with a highly skilled and motivated workforce.

Another major issue that the Soviet Union faced was the need to address the growing threat of the Western Allies. The Soviet Union had been a key member of the Allied Nations during the war, but tensions between the Soviet Union and the Western Allies quickly escalated in the post-war period. The Western Allies viewed the Soviet Union as a threat to global security, and the Soviet Union viewed the Western Allies as imperialist powers that sought to undermine its sovereignty. This tension between the Soviet Union and the Western Allies led to the development of the Cold War, which would last for several decades.

In addition to these economic and political challenges, the Soviet Union also faced a range of social issues in the post-war period. One of the biggest social issues was a shortage of housing. The war had destroyed many homes and left millions of people homeless. In order to address this issue, the government launched a massive housing construction program.

New apartment buildings were constructed throughout the country, providing much-needed housing for the Soviet people.

Another social issue that the Soviet Union faced was a shortage of food. The war had devastated the country's agricultural sector, and it was difficult to produce enough food to meet the needs of the population. The government implemented a series of agricultural reforms, including the collectivization of farms and the introduction of new farming techniques, in order to address this issue. These reforms were successful, and the country was able to produce enough food to meet the needs of its citizens.

One of the most significant social issues that the Soviet Union faced after World War II was the issue of war trauma. Millions of Soviet soldiers had fought and died in the war, and those who survived often struggled with the physical and psychological scars of the conflict. The government implemented a number of programs aimed at providing medical care and support for war veterans, as well as promoting national pride and patriotism in the wake of the war.

The Soviet Union also faced social issues related to its diverse population. The country was home to a number of different ethnic groups, each with its own unique culture and traditions. The government implemented policies aimed at promoting unity and cooperation among these groups, while also respecting their individual identities. However, tensions between different ethnic groups sometimes erupted into violence, particularly in the aftermath of the war.

Another social issue that the Soviet Union faced was the issue of gender inequality. While the government had made significant strides in promoting gender equality before the war, many women found themselves relegated to traditional roles after the conflict. The government implemented a series of policies aimed at promoting gender equality, including increased access to education and job opportunities for women.

Finally, the Soviet Union faced social issues related to political repression. The government was determined to maintain tight control over the population, and dissent was not tolerated.

Those who spoke out against the government or challenged its policies were often subjected to harsh punishments, including imprisonment or even execution. The government also maintained a vast network of secret police and informants, which created an atmosphere of fear and suspicion among the population.

The war had taken a heavy toll on the Soviet people, and many had lost loved ones or been displaced from their homes. The Soviet government worked to address these issues by implementing social welfare programs and providing housing and other resources to those in need.

USA

After the end of World War II, the United States found itself in a unique position as one of the most powerful nations in the world. The country had emerged from the war with a strong economy and a reputation as a global leader. However, the aftermath of the war also presented a number of challenges and social issues that the country would need to address in the coming years.

One of the biggest social issues facing the United States after World War II was the issue of racial inequality. Despite the sacrifices made by African American soldiers during the war, segregation and discrimination remained rampant in many parts of the country. The civil rights movement, which had been gaining momentum in the years leading up to the war, intensified in the post-war era as African Americans and their allies pushed for equal rights and an end to segregation.

Another social issue that the United States faced after World War II was the issue of gender inequality. While women had played a vital role in the war effort, many were forced to return to traditional roles in the home and workplace after the war. The feminist movement, which had also been gaining momentum before the war, continued to fight for equal rights and opportunities for women in all areas of life.

The United States also faced significant economic challenges in the post-war era. The country had experienced a boom during the war as it ramped up production to support the war effort, but this production could not be sustained indefinitely.

The government implemented a number of policies aimed at stimulating the economy and promoting growth, including the GI Bill, which provided education and housing benefits to returning veterans.

By utilising this war production growth, the USA introduced the Marshall Plan, officially known as the European Recovery Program, was named after US Secretary of State George Marshall. The plan was announced in June 1947 and provided economic assistance to Western Europe, with the goal of promoting economic recovery and stability. The plan was a response to the growing threat of communism in Europe, and was seen as a way to prevent the spread of Soviet influence.

The Marshall Plan was a massive undertaking. Over the course of four years, the United States provided over $13 billion in aid to 16 different countries. The aid was provided in the form of food, fuel, and other resources, as well as technical assistance and funding for infrastructure projects. The goal was to jumpstart economic growth and promote stability in Europe, while also helping to rebuild the continent's shattered infrastructure.

The impact of the Marshall Plan was significant. The aid provided by the United States helped to rebuild Europe's infrastructure, jumpstart economic growth, and provide stability in the face of the growing threat of communism. The plan was also seen as a symbol of American generosity and leadership, and helped to cement the United States' role as a global superpower.

However, the Marshall Plan was not without controversy. Some criticised the plan as being motivated by American self-interest, rather than a genuine desire to help Europe. Others argued that the plan would simply prop up existing capitalist systems, rather than promoting real change and progress in the region.

Despite these criticisms, the Marshall Plan was largely seen as a success. The aid provided by the United States helped to rebuild Europe's infrastructure and jumpstart economic growth, which in turn helped to prevent the spread of communism. The plan also helped to foster a sense of cooperation and unity among the countries of Western Europe, which would lay the foundation for the creation of the European Union in the years to come.

In the years following the Marshall Plan, Europe experienced a period of rapid economic growth and development. The aid provided by the United States helped to rebuild the continent's infrastructure, promote innovation and technology, and create jobs and economic opportunities. This growth and development would set the stage for decades of prosperity and progress in Europe.

The United States also faced a number of foreign policy challenges in the post-war era. The country emerged from the war as a global superpower, and it was responsible for maintaining stability and promoting democracy around the world. This led to a number of conflicts and interventions, including the Korean War and the Vietnam War, which would shape the country's foreign policy for years to come.

Despite these challenges, the United States was able to make significant progress in the post-war era. The country experienced a period of rapid economic growth and technological advancement, as well as significant social and political change.

The civil rights and feminist movements made significant gains, while the country's foreign policy helped to promote peace and stability around the world.

BRITAIN

In 1945, Britain had emerged from the war victorious, but the cost had been high. The war had left the country devastated, with much of its infrastructure destroyed and its economy in shambles. The country faced significant challenges in the post-war period, as it worked to rebuild and recover from the devastating effects of the war.

One of the most pressing issues facing post-war Britain was the state of its economy. The war had left the country heavily indebted, with a significant budget deficit and high levels of inflation. The country also faced significant shortages of goods and services, as resources had been redirected towards the war effort. In order to address these issues, the government implemented a series of austerity measures, aimed at reducing spending and balancing the budget.

The austerity measures were met with mixed reactions. Many people were willing to make sacrifices in order to rebuild the country, but others felt that the measures were too severe and unfairly targeted the working class. There were also concerns about the impact of the measures on the country's social safety net, as welfare programs were cut in order to reduce government spending.

Despite these challenges, Britain was able to experience significant economic growth in the post-war period, thanks in part to government policies and the resilience of the British people.

One of the key drivers of economic growth in post-war Britain was the government's investment in infrastructure projects. The government recognized that in order for the country to recover and rebuild, it would need to invest in the construction of new housing, roads, and public transportation systems. This investment not only created jobs and economic activity, but also helped to lay the foundation for long-term economic growth.

Another significant factor in the country's post-war economic growth was the expansion of its manufacturing sector. British businesses had been heavily involved in the war effort, and many were well-positioned to transition to peacetime production. The government provided financial support and incentives to businesses looking to expand their operations, which helped to fuel the growth of the country's manufacturing sector.

In addition to government policies, the British people played a crucial role in driving the country's economic growth in the post-war period. Despite the challenges facing the country, people were determined to rebuild and create a better future. They worked hard, saved money, and invested in the country's future, helping to create a stable foundation for economic growth.

As the country's economy began to recover, it experienced a period of rapid growth and development. This growth was fuelled by a number of factors, including increased international trade and investment, technological advances, and the expansion of the country's services sector.

However, this economic growth was not without its challenges. The country faced significant inflation and high levels of government debt, which put a strain on the economy and led to calls for additional austerity measures. The country also faced competition from other countries, particularly in the manufacturing sector, which led to concerns about the long-term sustainability of the country's economic growth..

In addition to these economic challenges, post-war Britain also faced significant social issues. The country was still grappling with the aftermath of the war, with many people experiencing trauma and displacement. There were also significant inequalities in society, particularly in terms of class and race. The government worked to address these issues, implementing policies aimed at promoting equality and social justice.

One of the most significant social issues facing post-war Britain was the need to rebuild its healthcare system. The war had left the country's healthcare system in shambles, with many hospitals and clinics destroyed or severely damaged.

The government implemented a series of policies aimed at rebuilding the healthcare system, including the creation of the National Health Service (NHS) in 1948.

The creation of the NHS was a significant milestone in post-war Britain. It provided free healthcare to all citizens, regardless of their ability to pay. The NHS quickly became a source of national pride, and remains one of the most cherished institutions in the country to this day.

FRANCE

The end of World War II brought about significant changes to France's economy, politics, and society. Like many other countries in Europe, France was left with a shattered economy, a disrupted political system, and a population traumatised by the war. The post-war period in France was marked by a period of rebuilding and reconstruction, as the country worked to overcome the challenges of the war and establish a new, more stable future.

One of the most pressing issues facing France in the post-war period was the need to rebuild its economy. The country had been severely impacted by the war, with many of its cities and industries destroyed. The government recognized the need to invest in rebuilding the country's infrastructure and stimulating economic growth. As a result, it implemented a series of policies aimed at encouraging investment and promoting industrial development.

One of the key measures taken by the government was the nationalisation of key industries, including energy, transportation, and telecommunications. This allowed the government to control key sectors of the economy and direct resources towards rebuilding the country. Additionally, the government provided financial incentives and tax breaks to encourage businesses to invest in new infrastructure and expand their operations.

Another important factor in France's post-war economic recovery was the Marshall Plan. The United States provided significant financial aid to Europe as part of the plan, which helped to stimulate economic growth and promote international trade.

The funds provided by the Marshall Plan were instrumental in supporting France's post-war reconstruction efforts.

Despite these efforts, France faced significant economic challenges in the post-war period. Inflation was high, and the country faced a shortage of resources and materials needed for reconstruction. The government was also grappling with the issue of debt, which limited its ability to invest in new infrastructure and stimulate economic growth.

In addition to economic challenges, France also faced significant political turmoil in the post-war period. The country had been occupied by Nazi forces during the war, and many French citizens had collaborated with the enemy. This led to a period of intense political polarisation, with tensions between left-wing and right-wing factions in the country. There were also concerns about the potential for communist influence, which led to the government taking a hard-line stance against communist organisations.

Despite these challenges, France was able to make significant progress in the post-war period. The country's economy rebounded, with significant growth in industries such as steel, energy, and agriculture. The government also invested in new infrastructure projects, such as the construction of highways and new public housing.

CHAPTER XXVII: REMEMBERING THE WAR THAT CHANGED THE WORLD

As the world emerged from the devastation of World War II, there was a collective sense of both relief and disbelief. The war had been the deadliest conflict in human history, leaving a trail of destruction and despair in its wake. But it had also marked a turning point in global history, with profound implications for the future of humanity.

As the dust settled on the battlefields of World War II, the world was left to grapple with the aftermath of the deadliest conflict in human history. The war had claimed the lives of an estimated 70-85 million people, including civilians and military personnel. The destruction wrought by the war was catastrophic, with entire cities reduced to rubble, economies shattered, and societies torn apart. The legacy of World War II continues to shape the world we live in today, and its impact is felt in every corner of the globe.

The aftermath of the war was a period of transition and rebuilding, as nations struggled to recover from the physical, emotional, and psychological tolls of the conflict. In Europe, the continent had been left in ruins, with cities reduced to rubble and economies in shambles. The task of reconstruction was monumental, and it would take years to restore the region to its former glory. The war had also forced many individuals and communities to confront the horrors of genocide and racial hatred, leading to a collective sense of guilt and responsibility for the atrocities committed during the conflict.

In Asia, the war had taken an even greater toll, with Japan suffering the devastation of atomic bombs and the loss of over two million lives. The conflict had also marked the end of European and Asian imperialism, paving the way for the emergence of new world powers and the reshaping of international relations. The post-war era was marked by a drive towards international cooperation and peace, with the establishment of the United Nations and the Universal Declaration of Human Rights.

Despite these positive developments, the aftermath of the war was not without its challenges. The emergence of the Soviet Union and the United States as superpowers created a bipolar world order, leading to a new level of uncertainty and fear. The threat of nuclear annihilation loomed large, leading to a global arms race and the development of new weapons of mass destruction. The war had also left deep scars on many societies, with millions of people displaced, traumatised, and struggling to rebuild their lives.

The legacy of World War II continues to shape the world in profound ways. The conflict set the stage for the Cold War, the rise of the United States as a superpower, and the emergence of new political and economic systems. It also led to the creation of the European Union, the modern state of Israel, and the establishment of new norms and institutions for international cooperation and human rights.

As we reflect on the events and aftermath of World War II, it is clear that the conflict was a turning point in human history.

It taught us the consequences of unchecked aggression, the importance of collective action and diplomacy, and the need for compassion and understanding in the face of adversity. While the world continues to grapple with the legacies of the conflict, the lessons of World War II continue to inspire us to work towards a better, more peaceful future.

AUTHOR'S NOTES

I would like to express my sincerest gratitude and appreciation for taking the time to read WWII: THE DEADLIEST CONFLICT IN HUMAN HISTORY. By delving into the complexities and historical events of this era, you have not only expanded your knowledge and understanding of this pivotal moment in history but have also honoured the memory of those who lived and died during this time.

It is through the collective efforts of individuals such as yourself, who are committed to learning and exploring history, that we can continue to preserve the lessons and legacies of the past. By doing so, we can gain valuable insights and perspectives that can help us navigate the challenges of our own time.

Once again, I thank you for your interest in World War II, and I hope that the book has provided you with a deeper understanding of this significant period in history.

If you have enjoyed this book feel free to leave a review on Amazon!

NUREMBERG TRIALS

As the sun set over the city of Nuremberg in the fall of 1945, a remarkable event was unfolding. For the first time in history, high-ranking officials of a defeated nation were being tried in a court of law for crimes against humanity. The Nuremberg Trials were not only a legal milestone but also a profound moment in human history. They represented an attempt to bring to justice those who had been responsible for some of the most heinous crimes committed during World War II.

The seeds of the trials were planted in 1942 when Allied leaders, including U.S. President Franklin D. Roosevelt, British Prime Minister Winston Churchill, and Soviet Premier Joseph Stalin, issued the Moscow Declaration. The declaration stated that the Allies would hold accountable those responsible for war crimes and crimes against humanity. It was not until the war had ended, however, that the legal framework for such trials was established.

The preparations for the Nuremberg Trials began long before the first defendants were ever brought to court. The formation of the International Military Tribunal (IMT) was the first step in the process. The IMT was created by an agreement between the four Allied powers – the United States, Great Britain, the Soviet Union, and France – and was tasked with trying the highest-ranking Nazi officials for war crimes and crimes against humanity.

Some of the most evil men in history were about to have their most heinous acts broadcast to the world...

To Continue Reading For FREE Please Email:

"NUREMBERG TRIAL"

To "R.M.CHESTERPUBLISHING@GMAIL.COM"

Made in the USA
Coppell, TX
10 January 2024

27548823R00216